PAPERART

THE ART OF
SCULPTING
WITH PAPER

First published in the United States
of America by
Quarry Books, an imprint of
Rockport Publishers, Inc.
33 Commercial Street
Gloucester, Massachusetts 01930-5089
Telephone: (978) 282-9590
Fax: (978) 283-2742

Distributed to the book trade and
art trade in the United States by
North Light Books, an imprint of
F & W Publications
1507 Dana Avenue
Cincinnati, Ohio 45207
Telephone: (800) 289-0963

Other distribution by
Rockport Publishers, Inc.
Gloucester, Massachusetts 01930-5089

ISBN 1-56496-378-0

10 9 8 7 6 5 4 3 2 1

Design: The Design Company
Cover Image (also on pages 2 and 3):"Hummin in
the Meadow," 36" x 17" x 5" (1.5 m x 71 cm x 20 cm)
by Patty Tenneboe Eckman. Photo by Allen Eckman.

Artwork on page 5, "Kitsune Tapandbu,"
by Kyoko Nakanishi; page 6, "Japanese Crane,"
by Naomiki Sato.

Printed in Hong Kong by Midas Printing Limited.

See page 141 for full list of photo and text credits.

This book is dedicated to the
memory of Evangeline Rossi,
in warm appreciation for her
lifetime of friendship, wisdom,
and encouragement in the
spirit of Vinton Pond.

PAPERART

THE ART OF
SCULPTING
WITH PAPER

A STEP-BY-STEP
GUIDE AND SHOWCASE

*To the Fitchburg Public Library
with fond memories, from the Author.*

MICHAEL G. LAFOSSE

Michael G. LaFosse

11-2-98

Quarry Books
Gloucester, Massachusetts
Distributed by North Light Books
Cincinnati, Ohio

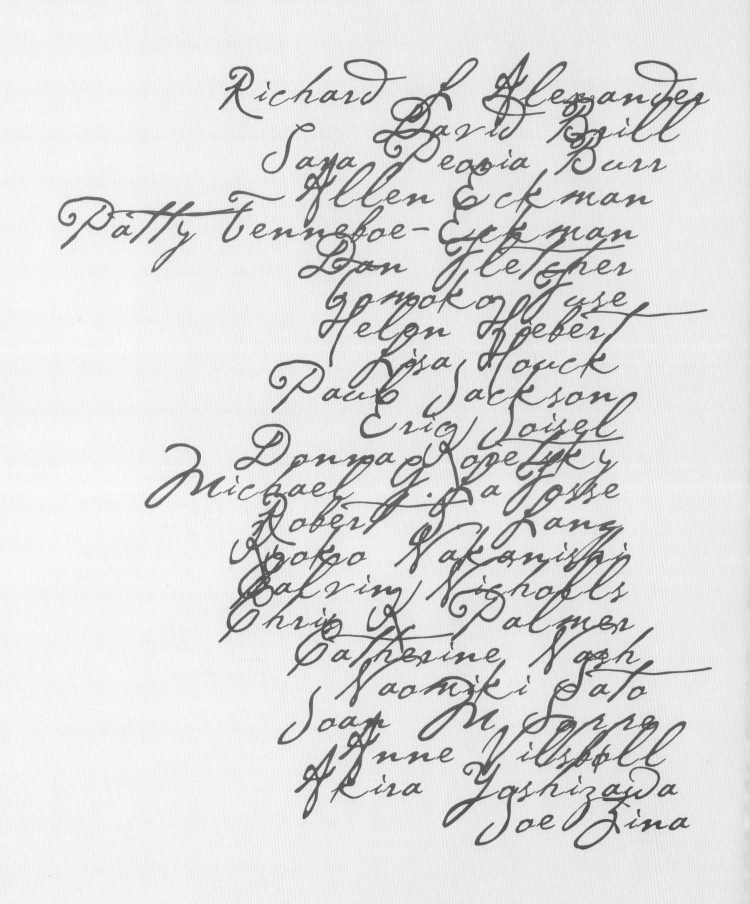

Richard L. Alexander
David Brill
Sara Peoria Burr
Allen Eckman
Patty Tenneboe-Eckman
Dan Fletcher
Tomoko Fuse
Helen Hiebert
Lisa Houck
Paul Jackson
Eric Joisel
Donna Kopetsky
Michael G. LaFosse
Robert J. Lang
Kyoko Nakanishi
Calvin Nicholls
Chris K. Palmer
Catherine Nash
Naomiki Sato
Joan M. Soppe
Anne Vilsbøll
Akira Yoshizawa
Joe Zina

CONTENTS

INTRODUCTION

If you love paper and working with paper, you will surely be inspired by the many fine examples of the paper arts presented in this book. The varieties of styles and techniques, and the high level of artistry demonstrated here are exceptional. Indeed, each one of these artists is among the best in his or her field. We are grateful for their generosity and we are honored to be able to present them to you in this collection.

Should this book inspire you to action, you will surely need some connections. We have, therefore, compiled an extensive reference section to enable you to contact paper artists, studios, schools, and supply sources. The World Wide Web is a wonderful resource for artists, so we have listed some useful Web sites for you to visit.

Artists enjoy communicating with each other on the Internet, and this has become a powerful means of creative cross-pollination. This is just one reason why the art of working with paper is flourishing.

This book celebrates this golden age of the paper artist.

Manufactured paper is a relatively modern material. Its invention scarcely 2,000 years ago was an important turning point in the history of art and communication, but until the last hundred years or so, paper was a scarce, handmade commodity. Technology and demand have developed quickly since then, and we are fortunate today to find an astonishing variety of high-quality, affordable papers readily available.

In fact, never before has the artist's paper palette been so rich—a richness that has tempted many artists of other disciplines to reconsider the new techniques, benefits, and opportunities afforded by working with paper.

SCULPTING WITH PAPER

There are seemingly endless ways to transform paper into three-dimensional artwork. To help you understand some of the common approaches to making paper art, however, the artists' demonstrations and galleries in *Paper Art* are organized into three basic categories—folded paper, assembled paper, and working from pulp—that are briefly described in the following pages.

These categories help to characterize each of the artist's work; they attempt to describe how the artists sees themselves in the context of paper art. Most of the paper artists in the book, however, draw on a combination of the different paper sculpting techniques to make inspiring artwork that is truly their own.

FOLDED PAPER

One curious thing about the art of paper folding is that people are always interested in how it is done, whether or not they intend to fold a particular model. For centuries, the art has been passed from person to person without the aid of printing or diagrams. Folding paper seems as if it should be easy, at least for the first few steps. Beyond that, you will need a communication system to properly remember, or share, a complicated sequence.

Over the years, origami artists and designers have developed a repertoire of folding techniques and manipulations. Just as musicians were compelled to create a standardized, printable language, origami practitioners have developed a standard notation system to explain folding sequences and ideas. This system of notation was pioneered by origami master Akira Yoshizawa, of Japan, and was developed further by Samuel Randlett, of the United States. The notation system is commonly referred to as the Yoshizawa/Randlett system. Since words are not necessary to understand the system, origami has quickly gained world-wide popularity.

Now try your hand at folding this model of a butterfly by Master Akira Yoshizawa. Use a small sheet of paper, such as a 6" (15 cm) square. If the origami system is new to you, the exercise will be useful before attempting the origami projects presented in Folded Paper. For a western version of the origami butterfly demonstrated here, refer to Origami from Nature, where Michael G. LaFosse demonstrates how to make a butterfly with more verisimilitude and more folds.

The basic key illustrated here shows a system of dashed lines and special arrows. The origami system of valley-folds and mountain-folds uses two kinds of broken lines (see diagrams) to show when to fold toward the project's surface (valley-fold) and when to fold behind the surface (mountain-fold).Various types of arrows help make the folding instructions even clearer. These arrows are easy to understand with a quick study of the illustrated key.

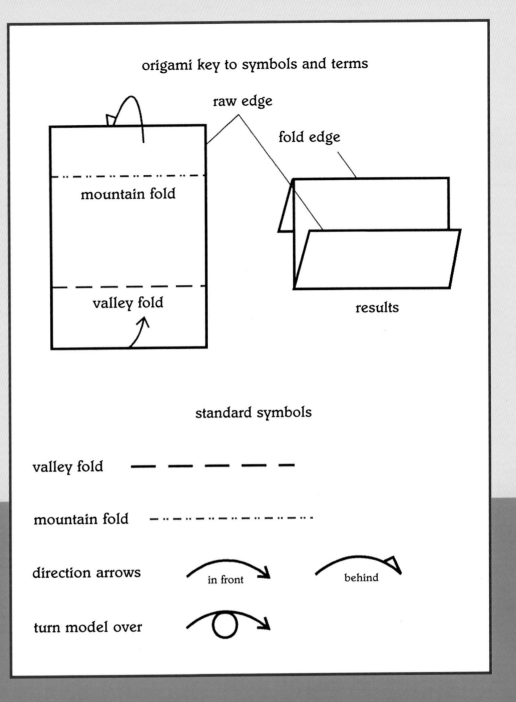

origami key to symbols and terms

raw edge

fold edge

mountain fold

valley fold

results

standard symbols

valley fold

mountain fold

direction arrows   in front   behind

turn model over

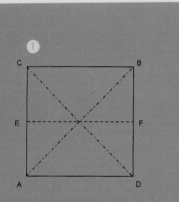

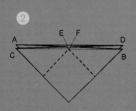

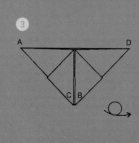

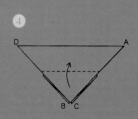

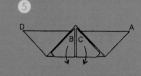

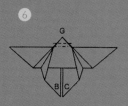

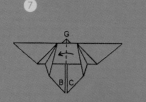

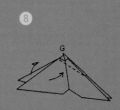

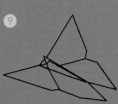

ASSEMBLED PAPER

Paper assemblage is where all the paper sculpting techniques—folded paper, papier-mâché, pulp paper—meet. There are endless ways to incorporate different types of paper, pulp, and even nonpaper materials. Each artist has developed and mastered clever strategies and techniques to realize their own vision.

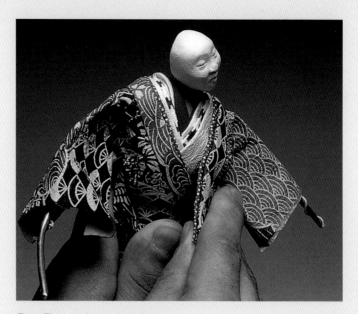

Dan Fletcher's *washi* dolls are elegant constructions of Japanese papers and clay assembled with wire and string. Often the papers used for the garments are the product of a special creping technique, which allows them to drape in a realistic, fabric-like manner.

Patty Eckman demonstrates the use of multicast forms to create delicate three-dimensional paper compositions. Each element was hand cut and shaped from sheets of cast paper. The paper elements are meticulously assembled using archival glue, and paper dowels or brass wire for support. White paper is a consistent element in Eckman's work—it purifies the work, uniting parts and allowing the viewer to focus on the sculptural detail, not the color, of the piece.

An example of pulp casting in an assemblage of paper fiber and non-paper elements. Catherine Nash has used traditional Japanese-style prepared pulps to produce thin-walled castings incorporating lashed branches. The branches have been webbed with an open weave material, which collects and drains layers of the pulp. When dry, the cloth is peeled away, revealing the cast, which incorporates the frame of the branches. Catherine combines multiple castings of various sizes and qualities to create commanding installations.

Joe Zina composes a collage with paper and fabric elements. He textures some of the papers with embossing techniques, then colors them with acrylic paints or printer's inks. Careful selection by color, pattern, and shape are key to him, and Joe keeps an extensive supply of materials to select for his work.

Lisa Houck applies colored, over-beaten pulp from a squeeze bottle to one of her pulp paintings. This liquid pulp contains formation aid, a viscous and slimy polymer that keeps the pulp flowing in an uninterrupted manner and prevents clogging of the nozzle. Such pulp "paints" can be applied with expressiveness and precision. Other colored elements in this composition are rather three-dimensional and add textural accents. They have been worked like clay, shaped by hand, and applied individually to the surface of the colored substrate.

Donna Koretsky sprays pulp into a fabric and wooden mold. The pulp is flax fiber and contains pigments, including luster types that will impart a subtle iridescent sparkle to the surface of the finished piece. Sprayed pulp is a versatile technique that allows the creation of large, seamless castings and sheets. Special equipment—an air compressor equipped with a suitable spray gun and a feed line or hopper to supply paper pulp to the spray tool—must be used. Pulps should be well hydrated to prevent clogging. All kinds of molds and forms can be sprayed.

WORKING FROM PULP

Paper pulp is essentially a blend of macerated vegetable fibers and water. Other additives, such as colorants, sizing, stiffeners, and formation aids, can be mixed with the pulp to create infinite combinations. Many factors, such as choice of fiber, water volume, and beating time of the fiber, contribute to the suitability and character of a particular pulp for any given application. These choices play an important role in the work of the artists in the Working from Pulp section.

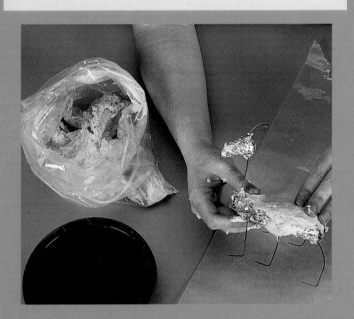

Sara Burr demonstrates the most immediate pulp techniques—papier-mâché clay formed by hand around a simple armature. The armature is composed of wire and aluminum foil and is shaped to the approximate final form of the piece. Celluclay, a paper pulp-based modeling material, is applied over the outside of the foil parts of the form. When dry, the sculpture can be painted and sealed.

Allen Eckman employs special molds, taken from clay sculptures he has fashioned, to cast his special paper pulp. A sponge aids in compressing the pulp, making it take the shape of the mold, and removing a lot of the water from the pulp. When dry and removed from the molds, each cast piece will be hand-finished, detailed, and assembled into the final sculpture. Allen's multi-cast system allows him to create a series of sculptures (as in works of bronze), yet leaves room for customizing to make each piece truly unique.

F O L D E D

Paper

Folding in paper is actually a three-dimensional drawing process. Creases can define outlines and textures, but they also create structure and sculpted form. Creases can be soft or bold, and the style of folding can resemble an orderly architectural drawing or a lyrical pastel sketch.

The appeal of folded paper is simple and innate: a play of surface texture, light, and shadow a tangible poetry. Paper is a wonderfully tactile substance, and so we fold it! Paper is irresistible: we automatically reach out to touch sheets of paper displayed in specialty shops, or fold and twist bits of paper or card held in our hands.

Shaping paper by folding is among the most immediate and interesting of techniques. There are many styles and strategies for creativity in the simple act of folding paper. In fact, origami artists produce astonishingly sophisticated and beautiful designs by folding only.

Whether the finished piece is abstract or lifelike, paper folding fits a sheet of paper, like a skin, around the spirit of an idea to realize the artist's vision. The work and techniques of the artists in this section are exceptional examples of this idea.

My greatest inspiration comes from nature, and I will spend days or weeks studying and sketching animals in their natural habitats before designing and folding an origami. After making initial pencil or brush-and-ink sketches, I work out the technicalities of the folds – which can take a single afternoon or several months. Having established the folding method, I create handmade paper for the finished design. Careful consideration goes into the relative thickness, fiber blend, color, and texture of the paper – so that the folded paper will appear beautiful and alive.

The origami butterfly project that follows demonstrates this principle of animation with copper leaf sponged onto handmade paper to mimic the gleam in the wings of a living butterfly.

"Most of my work is sculptural and not immediately recognizable as origami, but each model originates from a single, uncut square of paper."

Michael G. LaFosse

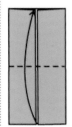

MATERIALS

- Black or dark-colored kozo (mulberry) papers

- Metallic or iridescent acrylic paint

- Acrylic gel medium (in a pastry bag)

- Crumpled wax paper or sponge

- Cutting tool (to trim paper)

- Bone or wood folder (optional)

STEP 1 Lightly dampen and then crumple the kozo paper so that you have a rectangular form that is somewhat smaller than the full-size sheet. With a damped sponge or a crumpled piece of waxed paper, daub acrylic paint randomly on one side of the kozo paper. Wear rubber gloves to keep your hands clean. Thin paint if necessary.

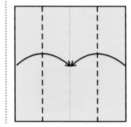

STEP 2 The overlapping paper in the creased area will have protected some of the base paper from becoming painted: Smooth out the paper to reveal the painted pattern. You can also try spray-on acrylic paint to decorate the paper. Let the sheet dry completely, then iron flat with the iron set on low.

STEP 3 Cut the paper into four small 6" (15 cm) squares. You can use the fold-and-slice method shown, or cut with a paper trimmer or scissors. Make sure that the paper is completely dry before you start or you will not be able to cut cleanly.

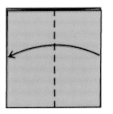

STEP 4 Begin with a single small square, unpainted side facing up. Fold in half, edge to edge, and open. This makes a center crease line. Fold the two edges of the square (parallel to the center line) to the center line. This forms a rectangle with a split layer of paper on top, as shown in the foreground. Fold this rectangle in half, short edge to short edge, so that the split is inside and hidden. The shape of the paper will now be square.

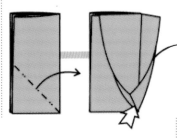

STEP 5 Fold the square shape in half, double-fold edge to double-fold edge. Open half of this shape and press it flat to form a neat triangle, as shown. Turn the paper over and repeat the process on the other side.

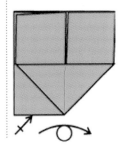

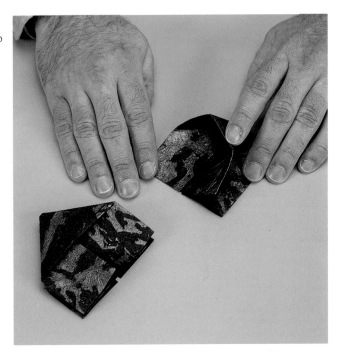

STEP 6 Open the right and left-side rectangular flaps from the middle layers and fold them across the lower triangular area. Look ahead at the next drawing to see that you are press-folding these layers to make the base shapes of the wings. Open out the layers of the lower wings, as shown, and press-fold the corners to flatten.

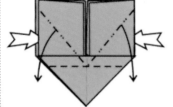

STEP 7 Follow the diagram arrows and fold the raw edges of paper marked, then tuck them under the folded edges of this area as shown.

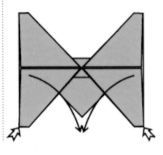

STEP 8 Mountain- and valley-fold the middle wing areas to create an overlap, fore wing over hind wing. Notice that the outside edge of the fore wing changes when you overlap it.

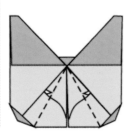

STEP 9 To form the body of the butterfly: Make a mountain-fold through the middle of the butterfly shape, as shown, then flank it with a valley-fold on either side. You can adjust the angle and shape of the wings for each butterfly. Repeat steps four through eight for each square of paper you have cut. Experiment with the folding of different kinds of papers and try reshaping the layers of the wings at various stages. You will discover many varieties of butterflies on your own!

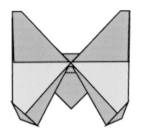

STEP 10 Apply a generous amount of acrylic gel medium to the underside of the butterfly body. Gel medium stays work-able for several minutes, so it is especially good for attaching and positioning three-dimensional art work. Arrange the butterflies on a paper-covered board and allow to dry overnight. Place as many butterflies in the arrangement as you like.

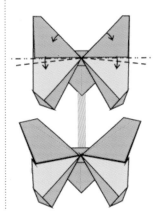

Kozo Butterflies
12" x 20" (30 cm x 51 cm)
Origami
Folded from handmade kozo-fiber paper with painted copper accents. Backing board is foamcore covered in handmade kozo-fiber paper with gingko leaf inclusions. Backing paper was tinted with yellow acrylic wash.

ARTIST'S TIPS

● Paper-covered foam core boards make fine mounting surfaces for origami and other folded paper art. They are lightweight and easy to work with using ordinary cutting tools, such as razor blades and sandpaper. You can mount these boards as they are, or you can frame them. ● Cut your paper 1" to 2" (3 cm to 5 cm) larger than the mounting board so that you will have some paper to wrap around the back side. Prepare your paper with a light spray of water before applying the glue. This will allow the paper to expand and relax a bit first. Applying wet glue to dry paper will cause exaggerated warping and possible damage to the sheet. Glue will spread easier on dampened paper and you will use less. Press out any bubbles that may form between the paper and the board, then wipe away any excess glue with a damp cloth. Allow to dry under light pressure from plywood boards to prevent warping.

● Choose handmade papers, which are strong and less likely to warp, for your backgrounds.

Equador

10" (25 cm) high.
Folded from a single, 23" (58 cm) square of Japanese moriki paper. The paper is solid black on one side, solid yellow on the other. The artist's folding method results in the yellow paper showing appropriately on the breast, bill, and eye areas.

Diving Pond Turtle

16" x 18" (41cm x 46 cm) Folded from a single, 19" (48 cm) square of French marbled paper. Mounted on paper-covered board. This turtle combines traditional origami with free-style folding techniques. To achieve the loose and expressive style of the feet, the paper is lightly dampened and folded. As the paper dries, the sizing in the paper sets, retaining the soft, graceful folds.

Praying Mantis

Life-size
Folded from a single, 9" (23 cm) square of
handmade kozo-fiber tissue paper.

Vermilion Goldfish

Life-size
Folded from a single, 9" (23 cm) square
of Japanese Leathack paper.

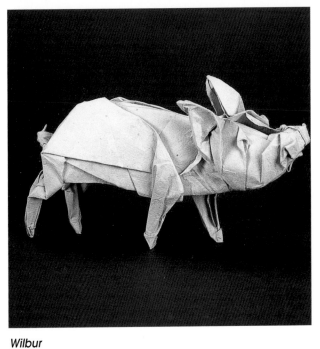

Wilbur

9" (23cm)
Origami. Folded from a single, 10" (25 cm) square of abaca and
cotton paper.

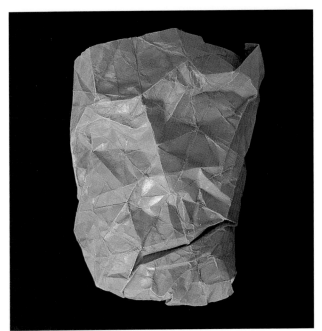

Portrait of a Friend

9" (23 cm)
Freestyle-folded 10" (25 cm) square manila paper.

TWISTS OF PAPER

After visiting Spain and being inspired by the tile patterns of the Alhambra, the palace of the Moorish kings in Granada, Chris Palmer made a mental connection between the tile patterns and the pioneering Hira-ori (flat-fold) designs of celebrated Japanese folder Shuzo Fujimoto. Following Fujimoto's example, Palmer embarked on a creative odyssey in folded paper, resulting in one of the most freshly inventive and dynamic developments in modern origami design.

The fascinating, medieval Islamic tiling designs of the palace inspired Palmer to develop folding methods to express geometric designs as radially-pleated tessellations. The most intriguing of Palmer's creations, the flower towers, do not have a specific three-dimensional final form; rather they can be twisted left or right, up or down, when pushed or pulled. For the past several years, Palmer has been applying these wonderful tessellation patterns to fabric, as well as to paper.

This box lid is an impressive combination of Fujimoto's basic twist fold with the traditional *origami masu* box. Many variations are possible, as is evident from the photos of Chris Palmer's flower tower boxes.

"I want to revivify the inspired designs that I have seen, and so I express these traditional patterns in the new medium of folded paper."

Chris K. Palmer

MATERIALS

- Medium to heavy-weight paper that is strong, but not too stiff or brittle

- Trimming tools: paper cutter, ruler and razor, or scissors

- Square box without cover

STEP 1 Begin with a square of paper the length of which is four times the length of one side of the box you wish to cover – a 4" x 4" (10 cm x 10 cm) box would use a 16" x 16" (41 cm x 41 cm) square of paper. Start with the under side of the paper facing up. Fold in half corner-to-corner both ways, then, fold in half edge-to-edge both ways.

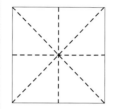

STEP 2 One at a time, bring each of the four edges of the square to the center line and make a short crease to mark the half-way distance between the edge and the center line.

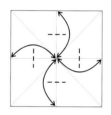

STEP 3 Mark the half-way distance between each edge of the square and the previous marks in a similar fashion.

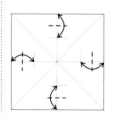

STEP 4 Define a small square at the center of the paper by bringing each of the four edges of paper up to the crease mark indicated for each edge. Only crease between the diagonal crease lines. Turn the paper over so that the display side is up. Notice that the crease pattern on the display side consists entirely of mountain folds at this time.

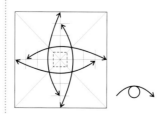

STEP 5 Install valley creases running from each corner of the small center square and parallel to the corner-to-corner mountain creases. You can make use of the four outer-most crease marks (parallel to the edges of the paper) to guide you and to maintain register.

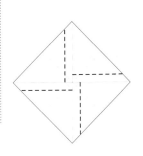

STEP 6 Use the indicated mountain and valley folds to create a twist in the center of the paper. The center square will rotate 45° degrees, and the paper will resemble a pinwheel. Turn the paper over. Notice that the under-side view displays a square area (white) with a colored triangle attached to each corner. Ignore these colored triangles when folding the next step.

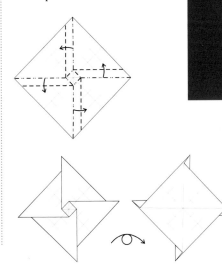

STEP 7 Fold a square corner (indicated by white paper area) to the center of the model. Then fold the corner (white paper) back to touch the center of the folded edge. Repeat these steps with the other three corners of the square.

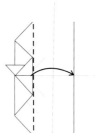

STEP 8 Bring the indicated folded edge to the first crease past the center line of the model. Unfold and repeat with the other three edges.

STEP 9 Tuck the triangle of one corner under a fold edge at the center of the model. A natural fold exists in the paper for this step. Use a similar crease on the other side to lay the opposing side triangle across the center line.

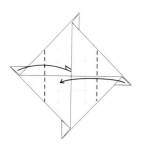

STEP 10 Pay close attention to the indicated crease pattern and begin to form the box, using valley and mountain folds. The right and left side walls come up first, then the mountain folded corners come inward, narrowing the sides of the pointed ends. The two pointed ends must tuck under the indicated layers inside the top of the box to weave the four layers together and lock them in place.

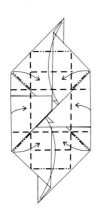

This view shows the last wall being formed as the final point is tucked under the inside layers.

Twist Masu Box
4" x 2" (10 cm x 5 cm)
The finished box lid fits neatly on the chosen base.

ARTIST'S TIPS

● To create box lids that will be durable and attractive, choose high-quality papers with strong fibers. Also, scale the thickness of the paper to the size of the lid — small box lids should be folded from thin papers; larger box lids can be folded from thicker papers.

● Be sure that your paper is trimmed perfectly square before you begin folding. This is important because the folding patterns are developed geometrically from the shape of the paper.

● To prevent distorting the crease pattern, take your time when aligning your folds. A small error early on can appear greatly magnified later. ● Fold the paper firmly to make well-defined creases. An elegant result is the product of clean lines and careful folding.

Iso-Area Flower Towers
13" (33 cm) square
Folded from a single 27" (69 cm) square of paper, with no cutting. The flower towers are plastic forms, capable of being flattened or pulled up. Several examples appear on Chris Palmer's box lids.

Hira-ori, Twist Octagons
10" (25 cm) square
Folded from a single 16" (41 cm) square of colored glassine paper, with no cutting. This impressive example of Hira-ori (flat fold) clearly shows the layering effect of this style.

Box Group

Three Boxes and a Tato

Left to right: Gold hexagonal box with lid; triangular flower tower box with lid, from hexagonal-shaped paper; gold pentagon box with lid; blue and gold tato box (a one-piece folded purse).

Hira-ori, Self-Dual Progression

16" (41cm) across
Folded from a single, ten-sided regular polygon of colored glassine, 20" (51cm) across.

Light Pattern (right, center)

12" (30 cm) square
Folded from a single 27" (69 cm) square of paper, with no cutting.

ORIGAMI PUZZLES

Paper artists and crafters will immediately recognize the ingenious hand of Tomoko Fuse, one of the most prolific and honored origami artists, and author of dozens of books describing her multidimensional, unit construction, folded projects. Each of her creations seems so natural that you might expect her to find inspiration under a microscope or in the crystal pattern of a gem. Few creators have such facile command of three-dimensional organization, proportion, and beauty. These multicolored works are also fun to fold! Because each piece is a puzzle, completing one of Fuse's designs earns you a sense of accomplishment that is both exhilarating and satisfying.

This origami quilt section is composed of the old and the new: Fuse's own four-pointed modular stars are joined by traditional Japanese base units, the design of which is hundreds of years old. To create larger compositions, you can add as many units as you like.

"All origami begins with putting your hands into motion. Understanding something intellectually and knowing the same thing factually are very different experiences. To learn origami, you must fold it."

Tomoko Fuse

MATERIALS

- Large sheet of paper, about
  8" to 12" (20 cm to 30 cm) square,
  for each center unit (use any
  quality or combination of papers
  for this project)

- Sixteen small sheets of paper, one-
  quarter the square size of your
  center-unit paper, for making the
  star units (mix solids with patterns
  if you like)

STEP 1 Starting with the center
unit, place the paper under-side
up. Fold it in half, corner to
corner, both ways. Turn the
paper over to the display side.

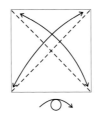

STEP 2 With the paper
display-side up, fold all four
corners to the center. Unfold
and turn the paper back over
to the under side.

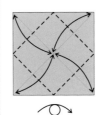

STEP 3 One at a time, fold and
unfold each of the four edges of
the square to the center and then
back out again.

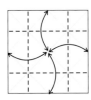

STEP 4 Fold the middle of
the edges to the center of the
square, then the corners in to
all. Fold with the crease pattern,
and the paper should collapse
easily into shape.

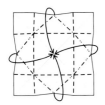

STEP 5 The display side of the paper is now on top. Prepare for the final step (pre-crease) by folding the raw edges of each square shape to its diagonal center line. Note: a "raw edge" is the cut margin of the paper sheet; all other edges are "fold edges." Unfold each of these pre-creases.

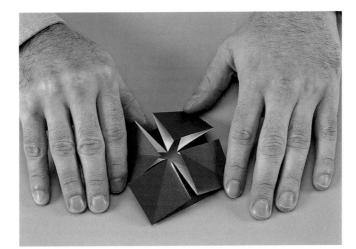

STEP 6 Bring each of the four center corners out, using the pre-creases that were installed in the previous step. This is the completed center unit. Turn the unit over to show the display side. You can attach up to four modular stars on one center unit.

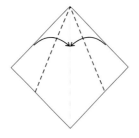

STEP 7 Each of the four modular stars requires four units and is folded from square paper that is one-quarter the size of the paper used to make the center unit. Begin by folding each square in half diagonally, then open the paper to reveal a diagonal center line.

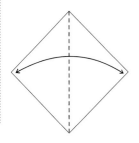

STEP 8 Fold two adjacent edges to the center line.

STEP 9 Fold to match the indicated points to each other and open the paper out.

STEP 10 You can now use this crease pattern to form the unit. Follow the drawings carefully. Make sure that you flex the lower-right triangle tab; this will make assembly easier and neater.

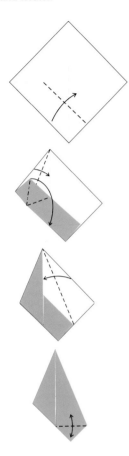

STEP 11 Assemble two units by slipping the lower-right triangle of one unit behind the layer point of the other. Be sure that the triangle tab of the inserted unit is free.

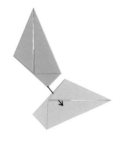

STEP 12 Tuck the triangle-shaped tab under the paper layer just above it. The tab should be completely hidden and the two units neatly joined. Add each of the other two units in the same way to form a completed star.

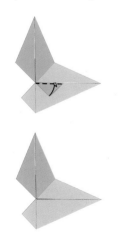

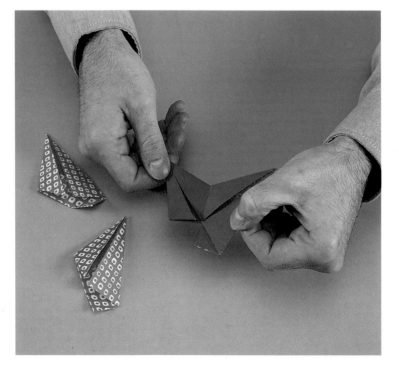

STEP 13 Assemble the other units to make a total of four stars.

STEP 14 Secure the stars by inserting the diamond-shaped corner docks of the center unit into the slit sides of the star arms.

Modular Origami Quilt Section

10" (25 cm) square
The finished quilt nucleus. This is the display side of the assembled piece. Additional center units and stars may be joined to this nucleus to create larger quilts. Tomoko Fuse has designed an impressive number of origami quilt forms using these and many other paper folded units.

ARTIST'S TIPS

• Papers should be trimmed accurately. Neat folding is essential for the pieces to fit together cleanly, so take your time. Try folding a few units from practice paper first. • Make a habit of sharpening your creases by running the side of your thumbnail against all folded edges. Sharply folded paper will give your creations a clean look, and firm folds will stay together better.

• When using a variety of papers, be careful about thickness—tissue paper and cover stock paper do not marry well. Best results come from papers that are of similar or equal thickness. You can, however, use a wide variety of papers: colorful gift wrap, pages from magazines, even junk mail. Paper is not recycled until it is used!

Origami Quilt
The major elements of this quilt are twist-folded square papers linked with simple blintz-folded (four corners to the center) squares.

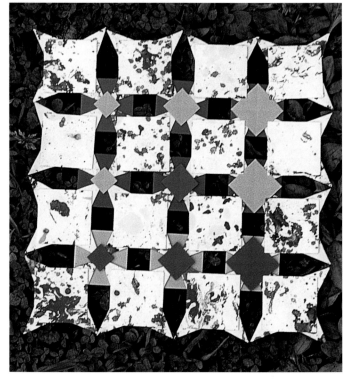

Origami Quilt
This quilt is created entirely from the folded form that was used as the center unit in the demonstration project. Non-petal folded units of various sizes were added to the display-side intersections.

Modular Origami Quilt

12" (30 cm)
The elements for this triangular piece are folded from
hexagonal-shaped papers.

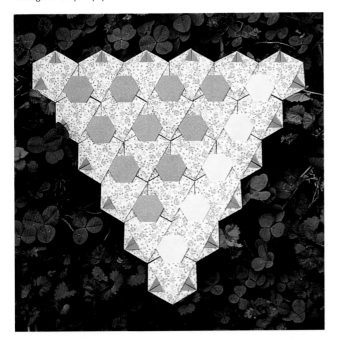

Modular Origami Quilt

12" (30 cm)
The triangular elements for this piece were formed from
hexagonal-shaped papers.

Modular Origami Quilt

12" x 12" (30 cm x 30 cm)
Each medallion is folded from a single square of paper.
The elements are linked in a technique similar to that
used in the quilt demonstration project.

Modular Origami Quilt

12" x 12" (30 cm x 30 cm)
This radial form was created from several different
sizes of papers.

All art this and facing page: Tomoko Fuse

BRINGING PAPER TO LIFE

It is impossible to imagine the expressive power of origami without first seeing the work of Akira Yoshizawa, the consummate master. The high level of artistic quality that he instills into his work carries through to his simplest creations. Full of life, they exhibit a vitality that artists in every medium seek.

Yoshizawa continues to demonstrate through his lectures, publications, and workshops the value of thoughtful study. He emphasizes the importance of developing and using a keen sense of observation, achieved only from hours of studying, understanding, and appreciating the wonder of nature.

This origami mouse, designed by Akira Yoshizawa and demonstrated here by Michael LaFosse, is folded in the air, not against the surface of the table. Yoshizawa believes this way of folding maximizes the expressive potential of origami. The technique of moistening the paper with water, a method Yoshizawa pioneered and has advanced through his teachings, allows the artist to make softer folds while preserving the integrity of the fiber. When dry, the object's final shape is permanent.

"I believe that origami carries the message of peace to everyone in the world. For when we use our hands effectively, our hearts are most at peace."

Akira Yoshizawa

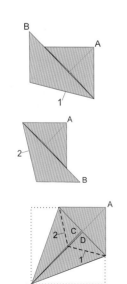

MATERIALS

- Art paper, medium weight, cut into 6" (15 cm) squares. The paper should be of good quality, contain sizing, and be colored throughout. Papers used for charcoal drawing are a good choice.

- Spray bottle filled with water and set on "mist"

- Terry cloth towel, lightly dampened

STEP 1 Lightly spray both sides of the square of paper and gently blot the excess away. The idea is to make the paper damp and flexible, not wet and soggy. In fact, the paper should look dry but handle like leather. Paper so treated can be folded with soft, expressive lines. You can use the dampened cloth to moisten areas of the paper that become too dry.

STEP 2 Before you begin to fold, imagine the form of a mouse. Keep this image in your mind throughout the session. Do all of your folding in the air; folding against the table will create a flat, expressionless piece. Begin by folding the paper in half, corner to corner, to establish a diagonal center line. Next, fold two adjacent edges to the center line to form a kite shape. Form pre-creases 1 and 2.

STEP 3 Now valley-fold the paper in half along line 3 while mountain-folding line 4, the portion of the center line that begins at the top of the kite and ends where creases 1 and 2 cross the center line. This is an inside-reverse fold. The paper will be valley-folded again along creases 1 and 2.

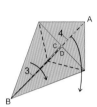

STEP 4 Inside-reverse-fold point A to resemble the photo. There is no exact placement for this fold. Each mouse will be different from this point on and will have its own personality.

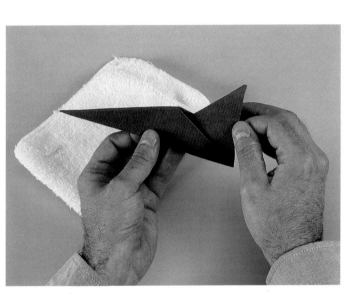

STEP 5 Inside-reverse-fold point A to meet with points E and F. Point A will become the mouse's head.

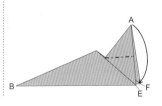

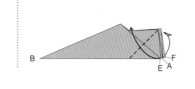

STEP 6 Position the paper for the mouse's ears by folding points E and F around the sides and to the top of the head paper.

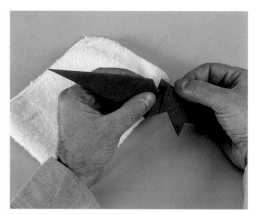

STEP 7 Fold the head paper down around the outside of the front, then inside-reverse-fold points A and B to begin shaping the nose and the tail papers.

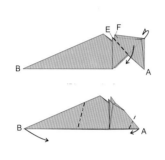

STEP 8 Inside-reverse-fold tail paper B back out a bit. Fold the lower edges of the head paper inside, for shape and proportion.

STEP 9 Open out and shape the ears. Apply additional shaping to the head if you wish. Narrow the tail by folding the lower edges inside.

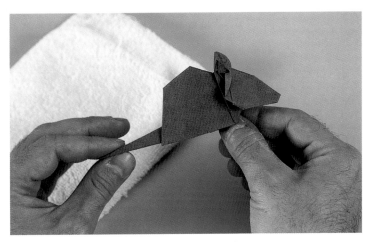

STEP 10 Round out the body and add expressive shaping. You can change the angle of the head or the tail. You can simulate the mouse's four feet by pressing a gentle arc into the lower edges of the body paper.

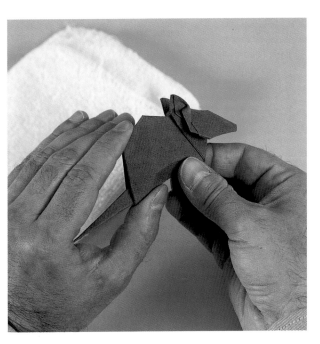

Collection of Mice

Each mouse you fold will be different. The angles of any of the folds can be altered for different effects. Try folding a small group of mice, each with a different attitude. Have some crouching to feed while others scamper about. The mouse can also be folded to appear standing alert, up on two feet. When you arrange the mice in a group, notice how each affects the other in the composition and how they seem to come alive.

Mice

These mice are more complex in detail than the example demonstrated earlier. Yoshizawa's creative techniques produce many styles of rendering a subject.

The World of Dogs

Approximately 2" (5 cm) to 10" (25 cm)

Yoshizawa's creative efforts in origami incorporate the study of variety in the natural world. Most of these dogs are compound models—that is, the front half is folded from one sheet and the back half from another. The challenge of this method is to maintain correct proportions and posture.

Crane
10" (25 cm)
This crane was folded with such precise balance that it is able to
stand securely on its own two delicate feet.

Self Portrait
12" (30 cm)
Folded from a single sheet of paper.

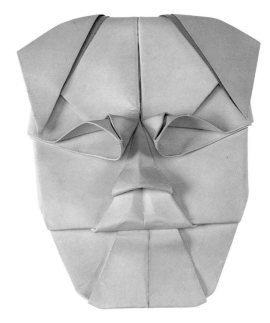

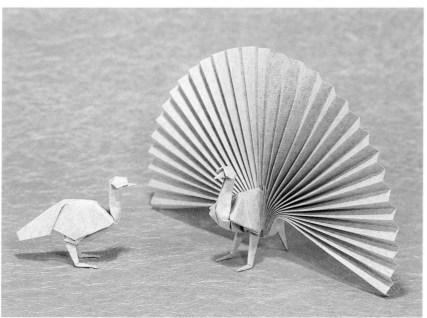

Peacocks
Male: approximately 12" (30 cm) across; Female: approximately 6" (15 cm) long
The tail of the male peacock is folded from a separate sheet that is added after
the bird is completed.

David Brill
United Kingdom
Double Cube Series
Each approximately 4" (10 cm)
Each is composed of folded modules
that fit together in puzzle fashion.
This display progresses from a simple
cube through the various stages of
an emerging, second cube.

FOLDED PAPER *Gallery*

David Brill
United Kingdom
Lion Family
Approximately 4" (10 cm) to 7" (18 cm) long. Each is folded from an equilateral triangle.

Eric Joisel
France
Mask
12" (30 cm)
Wet-folded from watercolor paper.

Eric Joisel
France
Mask
13" (33 cm)
Wet-folded from watercolor paper.

Herman van Goubergen
The Netherlands
Gecko and Fly
$8\frac{1}{2}$ " x 7" (22 cm x 18 cm)
Folded from a single square of paper.

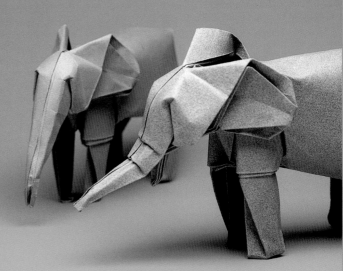

Eric Joisel
France
Rats
Approximately 7" (18 cm) long

David Brill
United Kingdom
Elephants
Approximately 9" (23 cm) long
Folded from square paper.

Paul Jackson
United Kingdom
From the Worlds Within Worlds series
Approximately 8" (20 cm) to 10" (25 cm)
Pleated and expanded papers. Finish is charcoal rubbed.
Each piece is pleated to form a tight ball, then pulled open
to create a hollow form.

Paul Jackson
United Kingdom
One Crease Form
Shaped from a 16" (41 cm) square watercolor board,
dampened before folding, and scrubbed with raw pigment.

David Brill
United Kingdom
Oxford and Cambridge Boat Race
Approximately 20" (51 cm) long
An origami rendition of this historic
event, which takes place every spring
on the River Thames in London.

Robert J. Lang
United States
Red-eared Slider and Hercules Beetle
Turtle: 10" (25 cm) long; Beetle: 5" (13 cm) long
Each folded from a single sheet of square paper
and no cutting.

Herman van Goubergen
The Netherlands
Cat
$5\frac{1}{2}$" (14 cm) tall
Folded from a right-angle isosceles triangle.

ASSEMBLED

Paper

An art form that truly takes advantage of paper's versatility, paper assemblage is the hub at which all the paper sculpting techniques— folded paper, papier-mâché, pulp paper— can converge. Assemblage combines or layers different sculpting techniques in a single work; artists use it to build complex projects.

Paper serves as easy collage material. Children know this art form well: From an early age, we all build with paper. Unlike constructions made of wood and metal, all you need to make paper assemblages is paper and paste. And with paper as a bridge between generations, industrious children and artists alike, armed with these humble materials, have a world of creation to command.

Paper assemblages often include non-paper elements. Joe Zina adds fabrics to his collages; Catherine Nash uses branches and vines for visual effect as much as for structural reinforcement; Patty Eckman creates finely wrought nature studies using custom-made molds and papers. Dan Fletcher's traditional Japanese paper dolls benefit from centuries-old techniques of paper preparation. Both Eckman and Fletcher employ armature materials that are not seen in their finished works. The possibilities are endless, and there are no rules to be broken. Regardless of the method or plan, each of these artists cautions one thing: Careful selection of paper or pulp is the key to success.

Patty Eckman and her husband Allen Eckman, whose work appears in Working with Pulp, use the "Eckman Method" of cast-paper sculpture. This process combines the use of their custom molds and forms with freehand sculpting of specially prepared "Eckman" papers. They have developed their materials, tools, and methods together and are widely regarded as the premier cast-paper artists in the world today.

Patty Eckman's art reflects a life-long interest in wildlife. She prefers delicate, graceful subjects, such as flowers and birds, both of which she renders with equal mastery and expression. Many of her delicate elements are first created from cast pulp and then hand finished. The final composition is assembled on a base form, either for wall mounting or for stand-alone display. The final works are rich in fine detail.

"We have really enjoyed the development of our fine art techniques over the years and have created a process that is worth sharing. There are many artists and sculptors who we believe will enjoy this medium as much as we have.

Patty Fenneboe Eckman

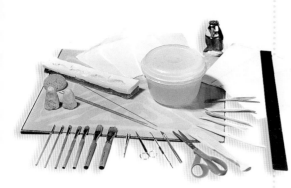

MATERIALS

- Molds
- Brass wires
- Foam core
- Scissors
- #11 craft knife
- Modeling clay
- Methylcellulose (prepared in water)
- Ragboard
- Tweezers
- Sponges
- Assorted sculpting tools
- Special processed Eckman paper
- Matteboard
- Straight edge
- Waterproof surface board

STEP 1 A mounting surface slab is prepared by securing together a matteboard back, a foam core middle, and a ragboard top. Methylcellulose is painted on the surface of the ragboard and placed upside down, then burnished onto Eckman paper.

STEP 2 Many "dowel sculptures" (an Eckman term) are made for the stems of the flowers with the help of a special dental burnisher. Eckman paper is torn into strips and carefully wrapped around brass wires by hand. Methylcellulose paste is used as a bonding agent.

STEP 3 The hummingbirds are cast from pulp using a custom-made mold. This process will be used to create the various insects and leaf elements.

STEP 4 A flower is built by first placing a short section of an Eckman paper dowel into a modeling-clay form. Flower petals are cut freehand out of the Eckman paper and then textured by scoring with a tool. The petals are then shaped and attached to the paper dowel stem with glue.

STEP 5 Flower heads and buds are sculpted freehand out of Eckman paper and wrapped onto a paper dowel stem.

STEP 6 Patty's leaf mold produces a sheet of elements that are easily cut out with scissors.

STEP 7 The flowering holly-hock plants are assembled.

STEP 8 The wing feathers for the hummingbird are prepared. The two halves of the humming-bird casts have been assembled previously and the beak made as a pointed dowel sculpture.

STEP 9 The bouquet of hollyhocks are arranged and affixed to the now-dry support slab. This is where work ends and the fun begins; this is the most creative part of assemblage art.

STEP 10 Finishing touches, such as blades of grass that are cut from Eckman paper, and birds and insects, are added. The molds and processes can be used again and again to produce additional works. However, each cast and assembled paper sculpture is a one-of-a-kind piece.

Hummers and Hollyhocks
24" x 22" x 3"
(61 cm x 56 cm x 8 cm)

ARTIST'S TIPS

- There are many kinds of paper pulps available today. For casting, the Eckmans like to use a blend of cotton and Abaca. Experiment to see which blend works best in your molds.

- Avoid warping the castings by making sure that the pulp has completely dried before removing it from the forms and molds.

- Use clean water in the preparation of your pulps. Water that contains high levels of iron, for instance, will likely produce rust stains in your paper. Check your water supply and use corrective measures, if necessary. The use of water filters can be effective; read the specifications on the filter before you buy to be sure that it will meet your particular needs.

Great Blue Heron Catch (Detail)
20" x 26" x 4" (51 cm x 66 cm x 10 cm)
The Eckman multi-cast technique allows for variations in each example of an edition. This piece can be done in three basic versions: fish in mouth, fish splashing in water, or no fish at all.

Hummin' in the Daisies
10" x 20" x 4" (25 cm x 51cm)
The delicate paper elements were built onto thin brass wires to create a resilient and easy-to-handle sculpture. The base was formed from acid-free foam core covered with handmade paper.

Red-tailed Roost
26" x 30" x 8" (66 cm x 76 cm x 20 cm)
Multi-cast paper sculpture.

In the Garden
18" x 20" x 4" (46 cm x 51 cm x 10 cm)
Multi-cast paper sculpture.

A Desert Tail
16" x 20" x 4" (41 cm x 51 cm x 10 cm)
Multi-cast paper sculpture.

COMPOSING WITH PAPER

Joe Zina, co-founder with Bernard Toale of the well-known Rugg Road Handmade Papers & Prints in Boston, Massachusetts, is a pioneer in the field of paper art. Zina is known for treating a single sheet of paper as a work of art, experimenting with inclusions into the paper such as flowers, sand, and confetti. His recent works include paper and fabric collages.

Demonstrating his strong sense of composition and subtle command of the medium, Joe uses stencils, embossing techniques, printer's ink, and paint to achieve a balance of textures and colors. Joe creates touch-tempting surfaces by texturing and layering his materials. To add richness to the collages, he often incorporates images created on a computer, output by a laser printer, and colored by hand.

"After years of creating handmade paper, making collages provided the opportunity to use all the papers that I had made. My work combines my passions for painting, pattern, and Japanese screens."

Joe Zina

MATERIALS

- Colorful, textured papers
- Colorful, textured fabrics
- Stencils
- Sponges
- Brushes
- Brayer
- Cutting tools
- PVA glue
- Adhesive film

STEP 1 A heavily embossed wallpaper is being customized with paint. Jar acrylic, thinned with a little water, is applied with a sponge. The first color is gently rubbed onto all surfaces, raised and recessed, to provide a solid background color. The second color is applied only to the raised areas of the embossing, allowing the background color to show for contrast. You can vary the pressure of the second color sponging to control contrast and density.

STEP 2 Another example of the embossed effect is achieved with a combination of acrylics and printing ink. The background is first colored with a solid wash of thinned jar acrylic paint. Gold printing ink is then applied with a brayer, which hits only the highlights of the embossing, producing a lighter accent and displaying more background than the previous technique. Printing inks are sold in paste form and are available in a variety of colors and finishes in either water- or oil-based formulations. To use them, transfer a small amount of ink to a palette with a putty or palette knife. Coat the brayer evenly and use it to apply the ink to your material.

STEP 3 Stenciling is a great way to customize your collage materials. Spray paints work well for this technique. Stencils can be adapted from found objects, such as screens or doilies, or they can be custom cut from paper, plastic, board, or rubber. Loose objects, in various shapes, can also be composed on the surface to be sprayed. Be sure that your stencil material is in good contact with the surface and that it is properly secured or heavy enough to prevent the pressure of the spray from dislodging it.

STEP 4 Creating textures in paper can also be achieved with a printing press. Here an ordinary piece of plastic screen produces an embossed grid design. The paper is lightly dampened and then placed on the screen. A sheet of newsprint is placed between the paper and the press felts; this paper absorbs moisture and aids in release. The embossed paper can be used plain or it can be colored, using the previously demonstrated techniques.

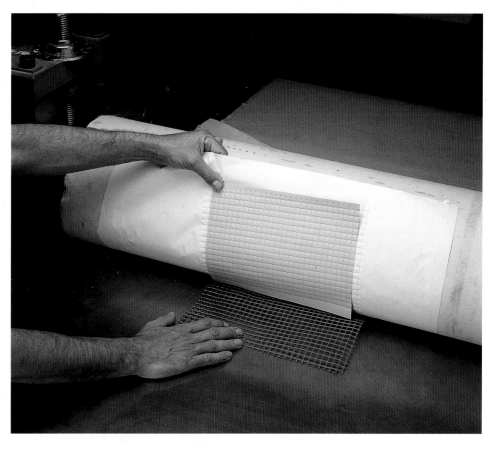

STEP 5 Applying adhesive film to the back of your material is best done before trimming. Roughly cut an amount of paper or fabric and place it on the exposed side of the adhesive film. A burnishing tool, such as a bone folder, is used to ensure good contact with the adhesive.

STEP 6 The adhesive-backed material can now be trimmed and shaped. A protective backing sheet covers the other side of the adhesive film. It will be peeled away before application. Joe applies PVA glue sparingly around the under side of the edges of the adhesive-backed elements. This added measure prevents the vulnerable edges from prying up over time.

STEP 7 Four-ply museum board is cut to size and the final composing of the elements begins. The process of selecting, painting, trimming, and arranging continues throughout the creation of a collage. Materials are not entirely secured to the board until the composition is established.

STEP 8 Joe's use of the adhesive film makes experimenting with these compositions quite flexible. Once an element is approved for placement, the backing paper is removed from the adhesive film and PVA glue is applied around the edges. The piece is then pressed firmly in place. The collage elements are applied one over the other, creating banded stacks of contrasting designs. Joe runs the final collage through the rolling-bed of a printing press to ensure permanent adhesion of the elements.

Antique Gold Peonies
11" x 39" (28 cm x 99 cm)
Paper and fabric on museum board.

ARTIST'S TIPS

● You can use contact adhesive film, available in rolls, and PVA white glue to mount your work on 4-ply museum board. ● After cutting fabric elements to their final shape, apply a small amount of PVA glue to the edges to keep them from fraying. ● Use only quality, archival adhesives for permanent works. Avoid rubber and spray cements; they are not archival and may stain your papers. ● Computer-generated images can be included in your collages. However, the dyes used in color ink jet printers will fade. Use black and white laser images and hand color with pencil or paint.

Red Victorian Rose
24" x 32½" (61 cm x 83 cm)
Multiple layers of materials add contrast and texture in this piece. Joe uses fabrics, as well as papers, in his work.

Red Poppies
33" x 34" (84 cm x 86 cm)
Cast paper and pulp painting on a gilded background.

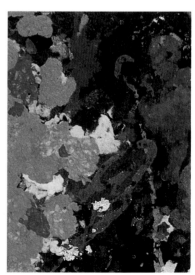

Gladiouluses (Detail)
Pulp painting
Colored pulps are especially suited to the creation of an impressionistic appearance. Masses of blooms, glints of light, and a background of greenery are deftly portrayed here by using pulps of various colors.

Man's Thoughts
39" x 11" (99 cm x 28 cm)
Collage.

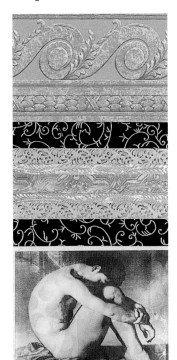

Winner Takes All
11" x 39" (28 cm x 99 cm)
Collage.

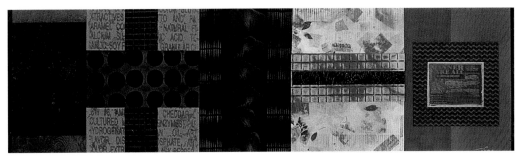

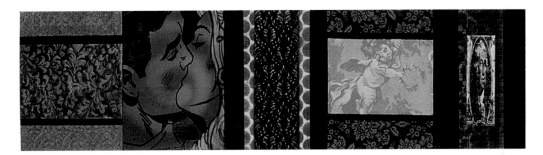

For the Love of Money
11" x 39" (28 cm x 99 cm)
Collage.

Orange Orient
8" x 39" (20 cm x 99 cm)
Paper, fabric, and hand-colored laser print.

WASHI DOLLS

*A*lthough the connection is not obvious at first, Dan Fletcher's background in the performing arts proved to be ideal training for the highly specialized art of creating traditional Japanese paper dolls, known as *washi ningyo*. These dolls, which often portray characters from classic Japanese plays, must be created by someone who truly understands the movement of the human body and its potential for expression.

Fletcher's early doll creations were promising, and during his trips to Japan he met several doll makers who offered advice and insight. One teacher, Kyoko Nakanishi, continues to be an important influence on Fletcher's development.

His dedication led Fletcher to an eighty-four-year-old master, Arasawa Eijiro, who agreed to teach him the demanding techniques for making *chirimen-gami*, the finely creped paper that handles like cloth. Today, there are perhaps only three other people in the world (all Japanese) besides Dan Fletcher who can make this kind of paper.

A *washi* doll begins with the careful selection of richly patterned handmade Japanese paper, or *washi*. The doll presented here is made of *momi-gami*, which is hand-crushed *washi*, and depicts a courtesan (*oiran*). Throughout the project, you will see that even though the figure is in a static pose, it conveys movement through its graceful lines.

"The use of washi, especially chirimen-gami, helps me to achieve movement and impart a sense of soul into my work. I wish to express my deepest appreciation to my teachers, who have unselfishly and patiently guided my efforts with a great understanding of their arts."

Dan Fletcher

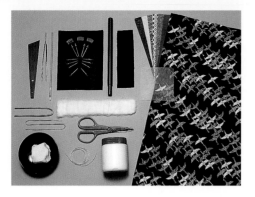

MATERIALS

- *Washi* (handmade Japanese papers): black for the hair; white for the body; and decorative for the garments

- Heavyweight aluminum armature wire

- Light-weight wire

- Hot-melt glue

- Surgical cotton

- String

- Glue *(konnyaku)*

- Air-drying clay

- Scissors

- Sculpting tools

STEP 1 An armature for the body is created with several pieces of aluminum wire. The highly flexible aluminum is bent into shape and held together with thin wire. Once the pose is right, hot glue is applied to the joints to prevent slippage.

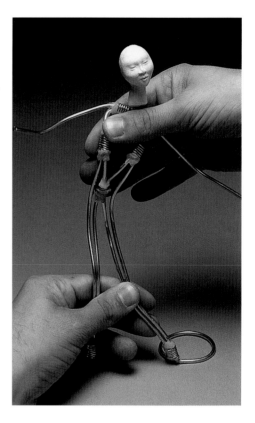

STEP 2 The body is wrapped with strips of surgical cotton, which tightens down on itself as it is wound. After a sufficient volume has been built with the cotton, it is tied down with string and covered with strips of paper that have been backed with the thick glue. The same paper and glue will be used as a backing for all the *washi* in this project.

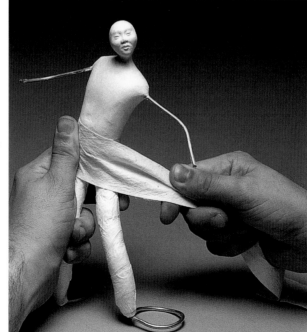

STEP 3 The head, which has been sculpted with air-drying clay, is placed over the top wire. The neckline and shoulders are sculpted and smoothed. Next, a very thin, nearly transparent paper is "painted" onto the face with *konnyaku*, a clear, gelatinous glue made from devil's tongue root.

STEP 4 The placement and curvature of the collars help to set the tone of the work. Notice the nape of the neck. It is necessary to give only a hint of color and pattern at the neckline— therefore, most of these collars are not attached to actual under-kimonos.

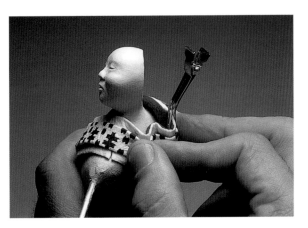

STEP 5 The upper-kimono is made by cutting out the neck and attaching the collar. Another collar, which matches the pattern for the under-kimono, is added, and the whole is fitted to the shape of the body.

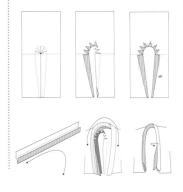

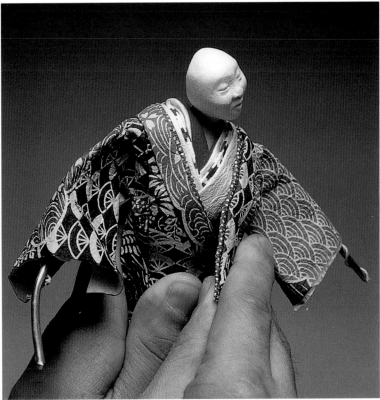

STEP 6 The lower half of the doll is made up of the outer kimono, its lining, and the layering kimono *(kasane-gi)* with its lining. The papers are backed, folded, and layered, and then wound around the waist of the doll and shaped. String secures these layers at the waist.

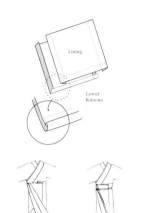

STEP 7 The sash *(obi)* is made of five pieces: the part that wraps around the body, the loop, the two free ends, and a small piece that acts as the knot. After the individual pieces are folded, they are assembled and attached to the front of the doll.

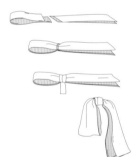

STEP 8 The longer parts of the sleeves are made with the use of a template to create a smooth curve. They are folded in two; the edge is glued along the bottom and half-way up the side, creating an arm opening. The back of the loop is left open. Small pieces of paper that match the kimono lining and *kasane-gi* are inserted into the openings. Finally, the sleeve is attached to the doll and given a sense of movement by shaping the way it drapes.

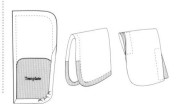

STEP 9 The hair starts out as a sheet of flat paper. Using a simple tool that consists of two plastic tubes, one fitting over the other, this paper is repeatedly crushed in one direction, giving the appearance of the "lacquered" hair that was common during the period of this type of piece.

The back hair *(tabo)* is formed first and glued to the back of the head. Next, the side hair *(bin)*, the front hair *(mae-gami)*, and the topknot *(mage)* are modeled and attached. Finally, the hairpins are added.

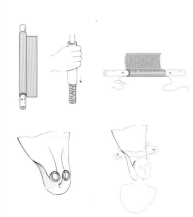

Oiran (Courtesan)
10½" x 8" (27 cm x 20 cm)

ARTIST'S TIPS

● Do your homework before attempting a *washi* doll. Traditional garments, the representation of their materials, facial expressions, and postures must all be authentic.

Courtesan
8" (20 cm) tall
Washi ningyo.

Courtesan (Detail)
The dark blue, patterned kimono is made of *chiri-men-gami* or creped paper.

Courtesan (Detail)
The flat paper of the towel contrasts with the *momi-gami* or hand crused paper of the sash *(obi).*

Okiku Tea House Girl
12" (32 cm) tall
Washi ningyo.

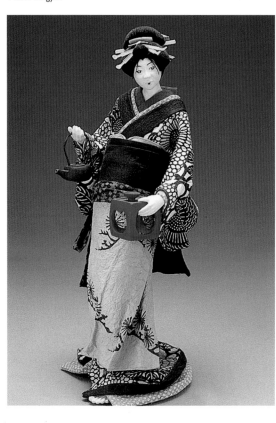

Townsman #1
12" (30 cm) tall
Washi ningyo.

Oiran (The Courtesan)
9" (24 cm) tall
Washi ningyo.

Tegami (The Letter)
5" (14 cm) tall
Washi ningyo.

Sharaku
7" (19 cm) tall
Washi ningyo.

Samurai
12" (32 cm) tall
Washi ningyo.

PAPER ENVIRONMENTS

Catherine Nash's installations are inspired, earthy works remarkable in their command of scale, as well as their solemnity. The qualities of fibers and the filtered light the paper creates lend themselves to the fabrication of intriguingly natural, organic places that invite exploration. Nash extends this concept by constructing environmental shrines or caves of paper over tree branches, creating shelters physically large enough to cover and protect the viewer, who becomes an active, emotional participant in the creation. Nash's works fairly beckon you to enter. The walls of these environments and installations are often back-lit, revealing watermarks, textures, crossing layers, and papers of various colors and hues.

This piece uses traditional Japanese methods of pulp preparation, which Nash studied in Japan under the guidance of Asao Shimura, paper historian and book artist, and Minoru Fujimori (known in Japan as a Living National Treasure). The qualities of the varied natural fibers and branches are coordinated through the devices of scale and form.

"My environmental installations are secret shelters that strive to recreate the sensation of feeling at peace with oneself and nature."

Catherine Nash

STEP 1 The pulp is prepared by cooking selected plant fibers and then pounding them by hand. Water will then be added to the pulp to create a slurry.

MATERIALS

- Pulp made from cooked and beaten plant fibers
- Formation aid, such as synthetic *neri*
- Armature made from thin and bendable tree branches, grape vines, basket reed, etc.
- Twine
- Loose-weave cotton fabric
- Needle and thread
- Staple gun
- Wood screws

STEP 2 Formation aid (synthetic *neri*) is added to the slurry. This additive slows drainage of the fibers and allows layer after thin layer to be built on the screen surface. *Neri* should be added slowly and carefully. Check the consistency by dipping your hand into the mix. The first sign of streaming threads rather than drips from the ends of dipped fingers indicates that just enough *neri* has been added.

STEP 3 Boat-shaped basket forms are created by lashing thin, flexible branches together.

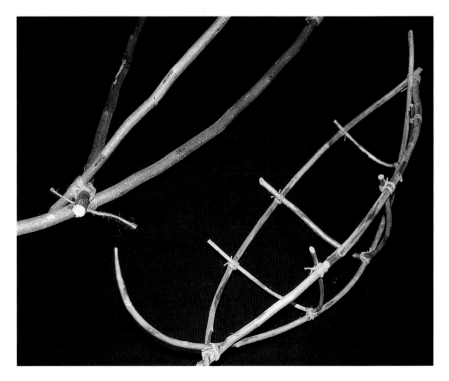

STEP 4 Tightly lash the joints of the forms with waxed twine or string. Soaking the branches before lashing adds flexibility and prevents splitting.

STEP 5 The joints of larger branches can be secured with wood screws. A pilot hole made with a drill will prevent splitting. The screws can be concealed with twine or paint.

STEP 6 Cloth is stretched over the outside of the basket form and is held in place with needle and thread or with staples. Note: Staples may leave unsightly holes. It is very important not to wrap the edges of the fabric around the inside lip of the basket form; the fabric will become partially embedded in the paper casting and will be difficult to remove.

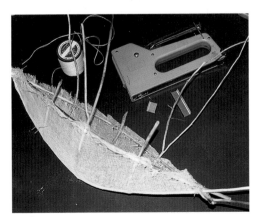

STEP 7 Inside view of a basket form with fabric covering. The cloth-covered form should be immersed in water for at least four hours before using. The branches will roughen and cause the paper pulp to adhere more firmly as it dries.

STEP 8 Pour a cup of pulp slurry into the mold. Keep the mold in constant motion to distribute the fibers as evenly as possible. Be especially careful to get the fibers down and around the branches of the armature to ensure proper adhesion. This first layer will form the outside surface of the finished casting.

STEP 9 Detail of a casting in progress. The casting is thickened by repeated additions of slurry, executed in the same manner. Be careful not to pour holes in the established layers; add slurry slowly and fairly close to the existing pulp surface. The final thickness depends on strength requirements and desired translucency. It is a good idea to form small separate sheets of paper from your pulp so that you have them handy in case you need to make repairs later on.

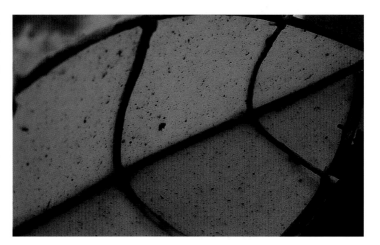

STEP 10 The outer fabric mold may be removed after the casting has completely dried. Clip the retaining threads and peel the fabric back carefully.

STEP 11 Leaves are added to one of the boat forms. Sheets of *gampi* bark paper are painted with watercolor paints, dried, and shapes are torn freehand. These leaf shapes are then glued to the exposed branches.

A total of five boat forms were created for this installation.

Nesting Boats

Lashed branches and cast paper. Fibers include cedar bark, torch ginger, *gampi*, *kozo* bark, and bleached mulberry. Cottonwood roots and grasses create the bottom nest.

ARTIST'S TIPS

- Choose casting fabrics that are loose and have an open weave. One-hundred-percent cotton cloth, such as fine cheesecloth or "India" gauze, work well. Avoid fabrics that are tight and smooth. Also, keep in mind the direction of the weave of the fabric; do not pull on the fabric's bias.

- Many mold shapes can be constructed for this type of paper casting—for example, bowls, boxes, and cones. Concave forms work best; convex forms can cause difficulties in casting.

- You can experiment with many types of plant fibers for your castings. Some fibers need to be blended with more reliable types. I have added a small amount of Abaca fiber to the torch ginger and cedar pulp for strength.

Homage to Magnani
Collaboration: Catherine Nash & Robert Renfrow
66" x 36" (168 cm x 91 cm)
Watermarked papers and mixed media. This cross-shaped light box, a collaboration between Catherine Nash and Robert Renfrow, was built as an homage to the Enrico Magnani Paper Mill, in Pescia, Italy, and to the artisans who kept the art of handmade paper alive for centuries. The mill, which closed in 1990 after more than 750 years of operation, specialized in producing fine handmade papers and chiaroscuro watermarks. The light box displays photos and watermarked papers in a back-lit environment.

The Clearing
22' (6.7 m)
Bent, lashed tamarisk branches and cast mulberry bark paper forms swirl in a back-lit composition. The artist uses a combination of traditional Japanese and Nepalese sheet-forming to create the mold for the cast-paper forms. Lashed branches serve as a skeletal structure over which muslin cloth is sewn. Thin layers of pulp are cast into the mold until the surface is evenly covered. When dry, the cloth is removed to reveal the paper form. The raku and pit-fired ceramic vessels contain colored sand from various Arizona sites.

In the Wind

Cast mulberry bark paper, branches, roots, and theatrical lighting.

Awakening

40" x 32" (102 cm x 81 cm)
Pigmented Abaca-pulp painting and mixed media.

Under Twilight's Dream (Facade)

10' x 16' (3 m x 4.9 m)
Environmental installation of sprayed flax fiber, straw,
branches, and theatrical lighting.

Under Twilight's Dream (Interior Detail)

Back-lit constellations are drawn with a jet stream of water to
create thin spots and watermarks on the wet sheets.

All art this and facing page: Catherine Nash

Kyoko Nakanishi
Japan
Yatsu Hashi (Courtesan,
Kabuki character)
18" (46 cm)
Washi ningyo.

A S S E M B L E D   P A P E R

Gallery

Naomiki Sato
Japan
Japanese Crane
8" x 6" (20 cm x 15 cm)
Cut and folded card.

Michael G. LaFosse
United States
Koi
36" x 18" (91 cm x 46 cm)
Koi are made from white watercolor
paper with red and black paper pulp
appliqué. They are mounted on board
covered with *Tosa Washi* bark paper.
Origami assemblage

Naomiki Sato
Japan
Owl
6" x 8" (15 cm x 20 cm)
Cut and folded card.

Kyoko Nakanishi
Japan
Othello (from Shakespeare)
23" (58 cm)
Washi ningyo.

Calvin Nicholls
Peacock
20" × 26" (51 cm × 66 cm)
Sculpted watercolor and printing
papers.

Naomiki Sato
Japan
Japanese Orchid Flower
6" × 8" (15 cm × 20 cm)
Cut and folded card.

Calvin Nicholls
Lion
20" × 26" (51 cm × 66 cm)
Sculpted watercolor and printing
papers.

Calvin Nicholls
Wolf
20" × 26" (51 cm × 66 cm)
Sculpted watercolor and printing
papers.

Joan M. Soppe
United States
The Memory of Knowing
6' 7" x 6' 7" x 24" (2 m x 2 m x .6 m)
Steel, glass, mixed media, and
handmade Abaca paper.

Kyoko Nakanishi
Japan
Kitsune Tapandbu (Kabuki character)
16" (41 cm)
Washi ningyo.

WORKING FROM

Pulp

Many artists who work with paper eventually find themselves standing at a vat of pulp. Only by scooping their own mold full of slurry and by hand-forming their own sheets of paper can they control the variables of texture, strength, and color to their satisfaction

Pulp is paper's most fascinating stage. It has undefined potential, which, in the artist's hands, can be molded, sprayed, scooped, and pressed into sheets, applied as paint, or modeled as clay. Because many elements are beyond the artist's control, there is ample room for magic and surprise. Each artist in this section has expressed wonder at this singular potential in his or her work.

Allen Eckman's cast pieces may be created as limited editions, yet each is unique because of his customizable multi-element construction method and the element of chance in the drying stage. The same is true for Sara Burr, whose brain pops are pulp sculptures, modeled like clay, over armatures. Burr uses no molds, and she paints her pieces. Lisa Houck's pulp paintings combine casting, modeling, and (sometimes) painting techniques. The drying process for Houck's work holds a color-change potential because colored pulps may dry to a different hue or color intensity than intended. Donna Koretsky's pulp castings are made from mixtures of fibers and pigments. Koretsky often sprays over-beaten pulp to a mold's surfaces, a technique that leads to high shrinkage and, therefore, a rigid and seamless form.

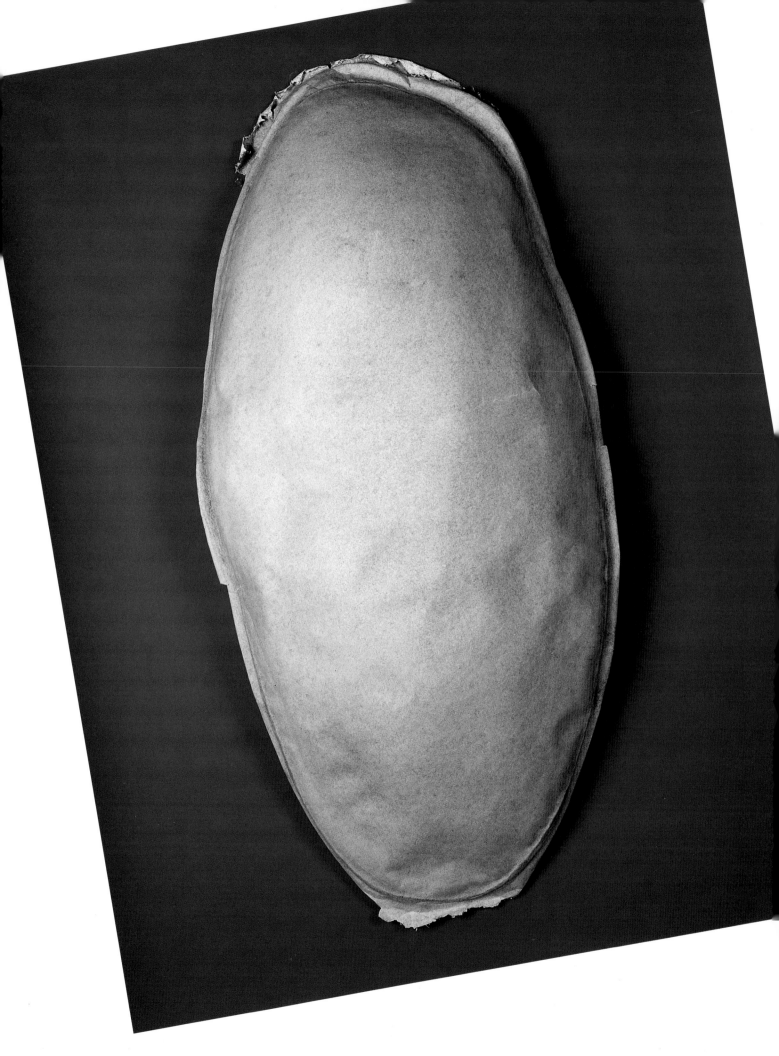

LIGHT FORMS IN PULP

Donna Koretsky's innovative work in paper reveals her family's important role in the study, development, preservation, and documentation of hand papermaking. Donna, with her mother Elaine, co-founded the first hand papermaking studio in Massachusetts, the Carriage House, in Brookline. Donna's husband, David Reina, is a producer of high quality papermaking equipment.

Koretsky's works in high-shrinkage pulp and luster pigments are alive with iridescence, yet the subtle textures make the simple forms palpable and monumental. The project demonstrated describes innovative techniques for casting and spraying large, seamless, organic forms in paper. The pulp-spray technique developed extensively by the Koretskys can also be used on flat surfaces to create huge sheets of paper or pulp paintings.

"I work with high-shrinkage paper pulp, restraining the drying pulp to disguise its weightlessness and fragility. These lightweight, hollow paper volumes appear as heavy and solid as rocks, shells, or other existing organic forms."

Donna Koretsky

MATERIALS

- Plywood
- Spandex fabric
- Heavy-duty stainless steel staples
- Clamps
- Wooden clamping strips
- Over-beaten pulp
- Formation aid (optional)
- Sawdust
- Saber saw
- Air compressor
- Pattern pistol spray gun
- Small sheet-forming paper mold

STEP 1 A stable frame must be created to support the fabric-molding surface. For this project, an oval is traced on a sheet of plywood and cut out with a saber saw. Feel free to experiment with other shapes as well.

STEP 2 Spandex, a highly stretchable synthetic fabric, is stapled onto the top surface of the plywood, covering the oval hole. The staples are spaced every few inches to provide even tension. Reinforcing strips of wood have been added to the edges of the underside of the plywood sheet for stability.

STEP 3 An air compressor and a pattern pistol spray gun are used to spray the flax pulp over the surface of the fabric. Six layers of pulp are applied. A short rest, about twenty minutes, allows the water to drain from the applied pulp between each application.

STEP 4 Small sheets of the flax pulp are scooped, couched, and pressed. These will be used to form a thickened rim around the perimeter of the form.

STEP 5 Coils are formed from the pressed sheets by overlapping the corners and rolling them up.

STEP 6 The thick paper coil is placed around the top edge of the mold. Segments of coil can be joined by overlapping and pressing them together, as you would when working with clay. Try to keep the diameter of the coil fairly consistent as you build.

STEP 7 Flax pulp colored with iridescent blue pigment is sprayed as a final layer on the inside of the cast form. This final layer will help bind the coil and cover any joints.

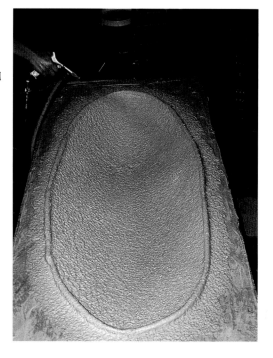

STEP 8 The inside iridescent surface of the cast form is burnished before it is covered, filled, and dried. Any smooth-surfaced tool is useful for this purpose.

STEP 9 A layer of Spandex fabric is used to cover the inside of the wet paper casting. This fabric will act as a release barrier between the pulp and the filler, which will be a 50/50 blend of perlite and sawdust. Without this barrier, the perlite/sawdust filler will meld with the pulp, ruining the cast.

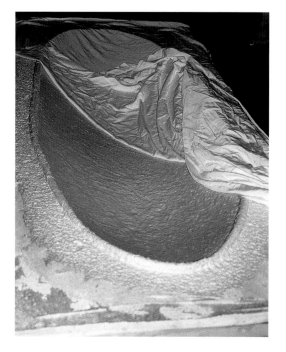

STEP 10 The void is packed with the blend of perlite and sawdust. It is important that the cavity of the casting be completely filled.

STEP 11 Finally, a plywood board is clamped on top of the mold, compressing the perlite/sawdust filler and keeping it firmly in place to prevent warping of the cast as it slowly dries. The cast is dry when it feels hard. A fan is used to facilitate the drying process.

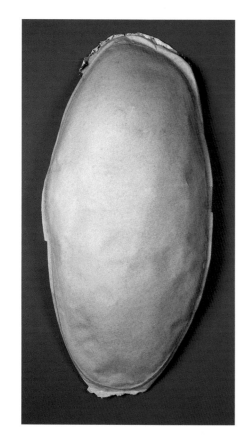

Study in Volume
The finished casting.
5' x 28" x 8"
1.5 m x 70 cm x 20 cm

ARTIST'S TIPS

● Pulp for spraying should be prepared in a beater. A minimum of one hour and up to eight hours of beating will give the pulp the proper consistency. The amount of beating time you use will depend on the amount of shrinkage you need and what type of fibers you use. More beating time equals higher shrinkage. Flax fiber tends to shrink more than cotton. ● The pulp should be smooth and lump-free. Pulp additives, such as formation aid (*neri* or synthetic *neri*), are helpful but not necessary to make the pulp clog-resistant in the spray gun. You may add sizing or stiffeners if you need greater strength in the casting. ● Use an air compressor with at least a 2-horsepower engine — more would be better. The higher pressure gives a finer and more even spray. Allow a rest period between each application of pulp (at least twenty minutes, more if using formation aid); water must be allowed to drain so that the pulp can set enough to receive additional spraying.

Trunks of Existence
7" x 7' x 7" (18 cm x 2.1 m x 18 cm)
Sprayed flax pulp, pigments, and wire.
Pigmented flax pulp was sprayed over the spiraled wire forms. The forms have been suspended against the sky using wire rods.

Knowledge (Detail)
9" x 14" x 18" (23 cm x 36 cm x 46 cm)
Bleached and unbleached flax. Over-beaten pulp was applied over the surface of a boulder-shaped sand bag. Once dry, the sand was let out of the bag and the fabric removed, producing a rigid and hollow form.

Around These Lines
7" x 7' x 7" (18 cm x 2.1 m x 18 cm)
Unbleached flax fiber.

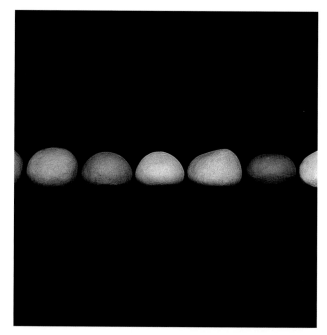

Dream Segments
1' x 3' x 2' (.3 m x .9 m x .6 m)
Flax, fiber, and iridescent pigments.

Shy Boulder
12" x 12" x 10" (30 cm x 30 cm x 25 cm)
Unbleached flax fiber.

All art this and facing page: Donna Koretsky

PULP PAINTINGS

Lisa Houck is a painter who began working with pulp at Rugg Road in 1987. The move from paint to pulp was a challenge. Pulp, a coarser medium than paint, produces a resolution that is less refined than paint, which makes rendering fine details difficult. Choosing design elements from her paintings, Houck creates bold, textured, brightly colored, lyrical, and evocative pulp compositions. Inspired by the real world, these other-worldly landscapes and shapes are hauntingly familiar, yet subject to numerous interpretations.

Under Houck's expert control, her patterns and forms translate seamlessly into the medium of paper pulp. She composes her work from a bright palette of colored pulps specially prepared by Joe Zina, keeping each color in its own pail. Once a cast support is formed, colored pulps are added in sheets, ropes, balls, and even from a squeeze bottle. These sculptural compositions are alternately built and then pressed on a vacuum table, which greatly aids in the de-watering process and helps bind the elements.

"My fanciful landscapes are filled with references to ancient cultures and the natural world. I look at the land from a pseudo-scientific point of view, with geology, archeology, and botany as sources of inspiration."

Lisa Houck

MATERIALS

- Pulp for casting the support
- Pulp for appliqué
- Pulp for painting
- Plastic squeeze bottles
- Molds
- Rectangular wooden frame
- Water-resistant foam core board
- Duct tape
- Bone folder
- Painter's shield, 2" (5 cm) wide
- Crepe paper
- Fresh sheets of colored pulps
- Small sheet-forming paper mold
- Pulp tub (to scoop sheets from)
- Felts for couching
- Papermaker's press
- Carpenter's square
- Tweezers
- PVA white glue
- Vacuum table
- Sheet-plastic drop cloth
- Brayer

STEP 1 The first step is the formation of the cast-paper support ground. Pulp for casting the support is made of two-thirds second-cut cotton blended with one-third bleached Abaca; sizing was added for rigidity and bonding strength. On the draining screen of the vacuum table, a $\frac{1}{2}$ inch (1 cm) thick layer of this blended paper pulp is poured into the wooden frame and patted in place by hand. The frame is then removed. The wet pulp should be lightly compacted and will keep its shape.

STEP 2 The serrated mold is placed at the top edge of the pulp rectangle and filled with an equal level of blended paper pulp. The new pulp is patted down and the mold removed. This cast pulp form will serve as the support ground for the colored pulp art. Sheet plastic is placed over the vacuum table and the vacuum applied to the form. Vacuuming continues for several minutes as the brayer is rolled over the surface of the plastic, evening out the thickness of the white pulp form and compressing the fibers.

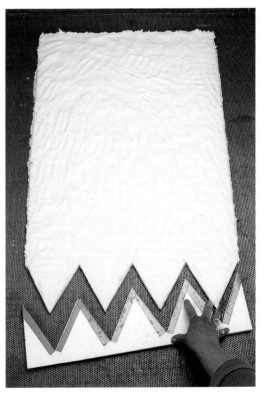

STEP 3 After vacuuming, the cast-pulp support is inspected and squared-up. Sheets of colored pulp are formed and then couched directly on the support ground from the mold, creating colored fields to work on. Other sheets are formed, couched onto felts, and pressed. These will be torn into small pieces for appliqué. The pulp for the appliqué is made of two-thirds second-cut cotton blended with one-third bleached Abaca; sizing was also added. Colors were achieved with pigments and a retention agent.

STEP 4 Gentle pressure with the metal edge of a painter's shield, pushed straight down into the white pulp base, define zones to be colored. Crepe paper tape protects previously colored zones from contamination by any newly applied pulp. The tape pulls away easily and can be used to fold the rough edges back onto the colored zone, forming a neatly folded edge. Raw edges of pulp, which run over the margins of the support ground, are folded to the back side, covering and coloring the white edges of the form. A few minutes of vacuuming and pressing are done again at this stage. Edges are then squared up with a bone folder and the painter's shield. The background is now ready for the pulp appliqué.

STEP 5 Here, colored pulp ropes and beads are being applied. First, shapes are lightly drawn into the wet surface of the colored pulp with the pointed end of the bone folder. PVA white glue is then traced onto these outlines. The PVA is important for the proper adhesion of heavy appliqués. Location points for the beads are similarly pressed into the pulp ground and PVA is applied. Pulp ropes and beads are formed from concentrated lumps of colored pulps and applied on the PVA glue lines.

STEP 6 Another pulp appliqué technique uses torn, freshly formed, and pressed pulp sheets. Tiny bits are placed randomly over solid colored areas. No PVA glue is required for this type of appliqué.

STEP 7 Pulp for painting is made with over-beaten Abaca, beaten for one-and-a-half-hours, with the roller down, close to the bed plate, to produce short, well-hydrated fibers; tororo formation aid was also added. This over-beaten pulp is then squeezed from a plastic bottle, creating lines and dots. The short fibers of the over-beaten pulp do not tangle and clog the opening of the squeeze bottle. The pulp has also been mixed with a slippery, viscous product called tororo. Tororo acts as a formation aid and is prepared from the root of the tororo-aoi plant. The crushed root is soaked in water overnight; the viscous liquid is strained and used in papermaking. Here, this formation aid allows the pulp to flow in a smooth, gel-like manner. The over-beaten pulp patterns should rest for a few minutes before final application of the vacuum table.

STEP 8 Before final drying and after the over-beaten pulp has set a bit, the pulp piece gets one last vacuuming to set the appliqué and to remove as much water as possible. A plastic sheet is once again placed over the project and the table and the vacuum applied. The brayer is used lightly and only on the flat parts of the piece.

STEP 9 The plastic is removed and the piece is squared-up and carefully inspected. Final drying will take place in a ventilated drying box between blankets, blotters, and boards. The blankets will protect the surface sculpture from crushing, and the blotters will aid in pulling moisture out. The whole assembly is kept under pressure to prevent warping. Total drying requires about four to five days.

Botanical Experiment in the Mountains
35" x 22" (89 cm x 56 cm)
Pressed paper pulp.

ARTIST'S TIPS

● Larger pieces can be created by producing multiple-panel constructions. That way, you are not really limited by the casting frame and drying-box sizes. ● Though colored pulps look vivid and saturated when wet, they will not always look so bright when dry. You can re-pigment and revitalize a finished pulp piece with paint. Lisa Houck prefers gouache to acrylic because it covers well and dries to a nice matte finish. ● Working with pulp requires a lot of water, but there are hazards associated with this. Be sure that there is adequate drainage in your work area and that all walkways provide safe traction. Be aware of shock-hazard potential where electrical outlets and equipment (such as the vacuum table) are located.

Red Mountains
33" x 22" (84 cm x 56 cm)
Pressed paper pulp.
Patterns are created with a variety of pulp applications such as sheets, ropes, and dots. PVA white glue is lightly applied under the heavier elements to ensure attachment.

An Ancient Map (Detail)
45" x 30" (114 cm x 76 cm)
Pressed paper pulp.
By using a common design element, the artist is free to compose and invent. The curved-line and circle pattern in each quadrant of this "map," inspired by the contour lines of geological survey maps, is enlivened by various colors, densities, and shapes.

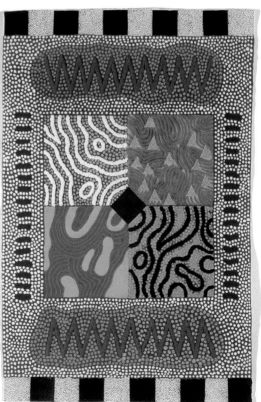

All art this and facing page: Lisa Houck

Snowy Peaks
33" x 22" (84 cm x 56 cm)
Pressed paper pulp.

Arboretum South
18" x 36" (46 cm x 91 cm)
Pressed paper pulp.

Trees of the Northern Hemisphere
18" x 36" (46 cm x 91 cm)
Pressed paper pulp.

Cosmic Map
45" x 30" (114 cm x 76 cm)
Pressed paper pulp.

Signs and Symbols IV
28" x 24" (71 cm x 61 cm)
Pressed paper pulp.

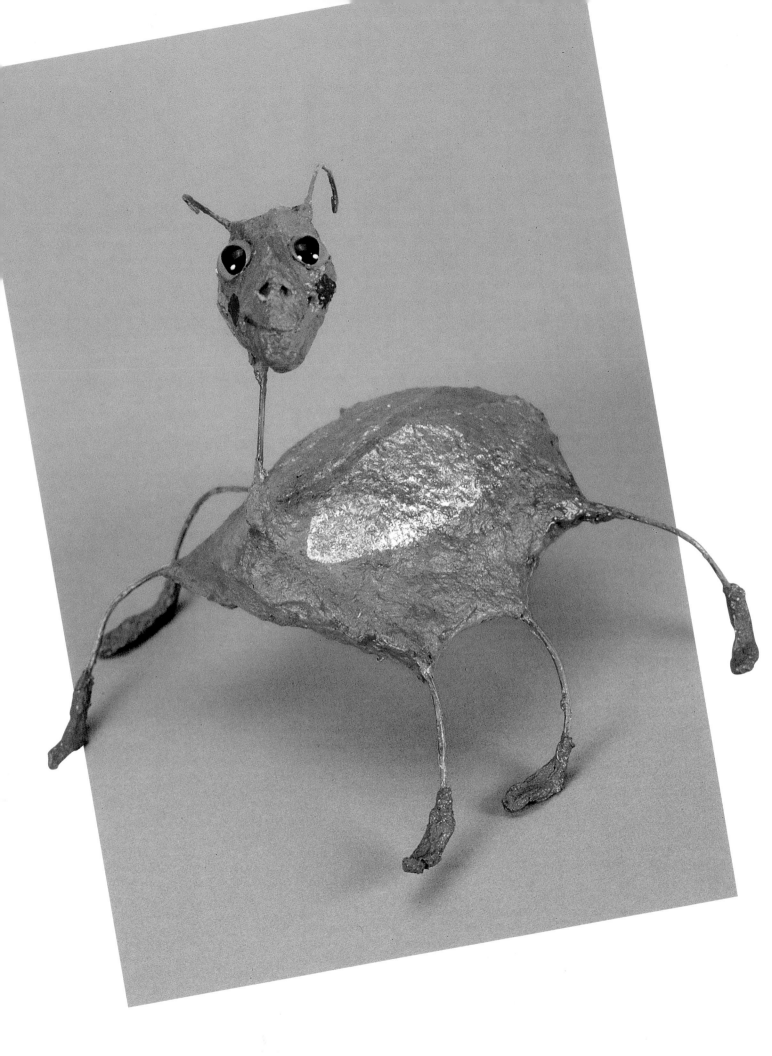

Sara Burr creates playful paper sculptures that evoke a vision of childhood. The whimsical spirit and life that she imparts to her work is magical. She aptly calls her sculptures brain pops, an appellation that is as off-beat and evocative as her work.

The creation of a brain pop can be an adventure. Although the techniques for building these paper characters lend themselves to duplication, Burr resists becoming trapped in production work. She looks forward to finding out what new beings will appear out of each bag of Celluclay (or commercial papier-mâché). Because the papier-mâché material dries to a somewhat different form than it takes when wet, even Burr can be surprised at the results. Some characters take on a little more sweetness or wickedness, and some even gain a certain glint of wisdom in the drying process. Their spindly, wire legs add a dimension of animation.

"I create brain pops because these are things that I want to see. A lot of the visual strength in them comes from a kind of dynamic tension, something I developed an understanding of from drawing. This tension elicits great reactions from people."

Sara Burr

MATERIALS

- Wire
- Foil
- Paper
- Paper tape
- Newspaper
- Celluclay II or commercial papier-mâché
- Water
- Wire cutters and needle-nosed pliers
- Craft knife
- Pencil
- Toothpicks
- Brushes
- Acrylic paints
- Plastic or glass eyes
- Wax paper (to protect surfaces)

STEP 1 Begin by forming the wire into a supporting frame or skeleton. Use paper tape to hold the wires together.

STEP 2 Flesh out the skelet on with aluminum foil. Foil is lightweight, easily sculptable, and is a good substitute for the papier-mâché material. Newspaper can be used to support the foil wherever larger volumes are formed, such as the body. Be sure to completely cover the paper with foil.

STEP 3 Prepare the Celluclay by mixing it with water and kneading it well. Burr prefers a consistency that is similar to bread dough. The material should be able to form a smooth ball and take detail from tooling.

STEP 4 Apply papier-mâché material to cover the armature. You do not need to apply a heavy layer, but be sure that the material is in firm contact with the support surfaces. You may want to work in stages, covering part of the armature and letting it dry before covering more of it, which is especially helpful when working on larger pieces.

STEP 5 Glass eyes are added; the point of a pencil is useful in forming the sockets in which to place them. Details such as the mouth and nostrils are formed with a craft knife and toothpicks.

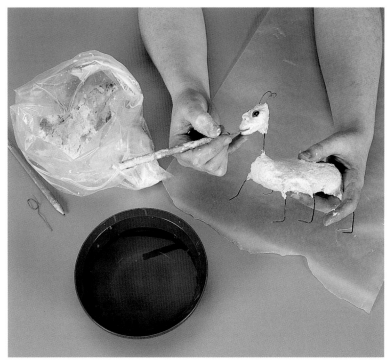

STEP 6 Painting can begin after the papier-mâché completely dry. Burr uses opaque acrylic paints for good coverage and durability. It is best to use a brush to apply the paint, especially if the dried papier-mâché is heavily textured.

STEP 7 Paint all paper-mâché surfaces to seal and decorate them. The artist also paints any exposed armature, such as the wire of the legs, neck, and antennae. Be sure that the position of each bendable element is satisfactory before you paint.

STEP 8 Additional paint layers and details are added only after each coat of paint has dried.

Brain Pop Being
4" long x 5" high (10 cm x 13 cm)

ARTIST'S TIPS

● Use just enough water to make the paper-mâché material plastic. Too much water can cause excessive shrinkage. High shrinkage can be desirable, however, if you would like a more unpredictable and wild drying effect, which can add extra character to a finished piece. ● Prepare your paper-mâché clay in a plastic bag; it is easy to knead the dough through the bag, and you can store the clay in a refrigerator for up to a few days. ● There are several kinds of papier-mâché products available. Burr prefers the whiter type of material because it makes a better ground for painting, especially if you use bright or translucent colors. ● After painting, you can finish the surface with an acrylic varnish or sealer.

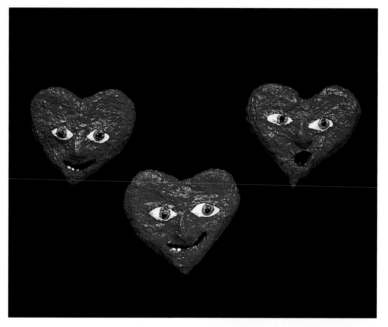

Brain Pop Pin Hearts (Detail)
Approximately $1\frac{1}{4}$" x $1\frac{1}{4}$"
(3 cm x 3 cm)
Small creations are perfect for making into pins. The basic hardware for the pin can be purchased at most craft supply stores. You can use hot-melt glue or epoxy to attach the pin to the back. Papier-mâché.

Purple Jogger, Brain Pop Being
10" x 10" x 3"
(25 cm x 25 cm x 8 cm)
Papier-mâché.
The expressiveness of Burr's creatures is a product of the sculpting of the forms, as well as the shrinkage and distortion that occurs during the drying process.

Orange Puppeteer, Brain Pop Being
9" x 10" x 6" (23 cm x 25 cm x 15 cm)

Blue Cat, Brain Pop Being
12" x 12" x 5" (30 cm x 30 cm x 13 cm)

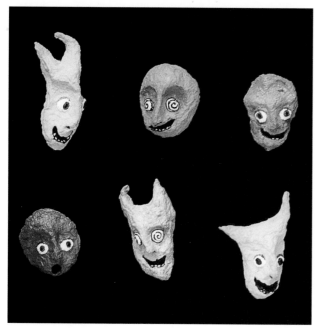

Brain Pop Pins
Approximately 1" x 1½" (3 cm x 4 cm)

HISTORY IN PAPER

Allen Eckman casts paper sculptures that depict Native American tribes, individuals, and artifacts. He has also begun work on a series of Civil War subjects. Research for authenticity is an important part of his art; his work is rich with ethnological and cultural detail.

Since 1987, Allen and his wife, Patty, whose work appears in the Assembled Paper section, have dedicated themselves to developing a new style of museum-quality paper sculpture. In doing so, they have invented a new process and a series of special tools. This accounts for the exclusive and distinctive quality of their work and makes it unique in the world of paper art. The Eckmans have protected their method until now, but they have decided to share what they have developed by offering classes, licenses, and equipment purchases.

This piece, demonstrated by Eckman, requires special molds and demonstrates the pulp-casting process. We suggest that the reader compare both Allen's and Patty's sections to gain a full appreciation for the range of tools, techniques, and processes required for the "Eckman" system.

"The paper has a mind of its own. Instead of trying to fix every little thing, I let things happen, and when the results please me, I leave it alone."

Allen Eckman

MATERIALS

- Paper pulp
- Molding silicone
- Foam core
- Scissors
- 35 mm film capsules
- #11 craft knife
- Modeling clay
- Methylcellulose (prepared in water)
- Ragboard
- Tweezers
- Sculpture stand
- Sponges
- Fiberglass materials
- Assorted sculpting tools
- Matteboard
- Straight edge
- Pins
- Waterproof surface board

STEP 1 A sculpture of the subject is first modeled out of clay. Here, Allen forms a bust of a man. Notice that the eye sockets are left open. The ears, eyeballs, and hands are sculpted and molded separately. Glass beads are also laid up for a mold.

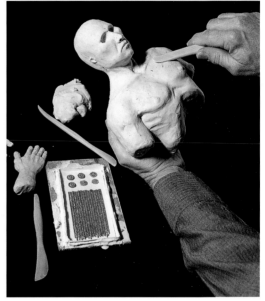

STEP 2 Shown here are the silicone rubber molds created from the clay models. Notice that the bust figure and the hand have been molded in two parts. A "mother mold" has been created in fiberglass.

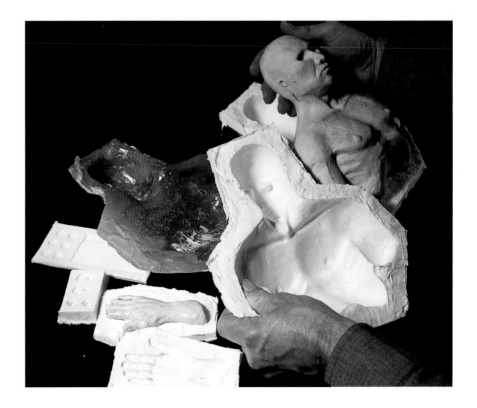

STEP 3 Pulp is applied to the inside of the molds by hand. Water is removed with a sponge.

STEP 4 The dry paper casts are now removed from the molds and the two halves are joined together. After further drying, a straight cut is made to accommodate a relief mount.

STEP 5 The relief bust is now mounted onto a slab made of matteboard, foam core, and ragboard. This lay-up has been covered with special, handmade Eckman process paper. Eyes, ears, and hands are added. The head is turned and the hand reposed.

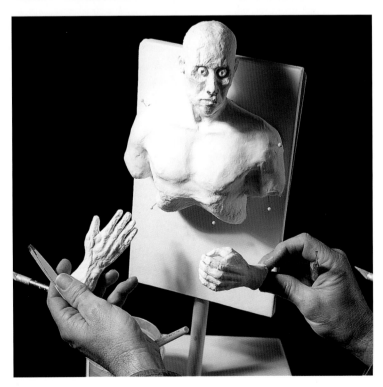

STEP 6 Small strips of paper are cut from Eckman paper. These strips are then scored and folded in half. The feathers are cut freehand from the folded strips. Spines and wraps are added, and cuts give the feathers detail.

STEP 7 A paper lance and shield have been fashioned, and the feathers are applied to each.

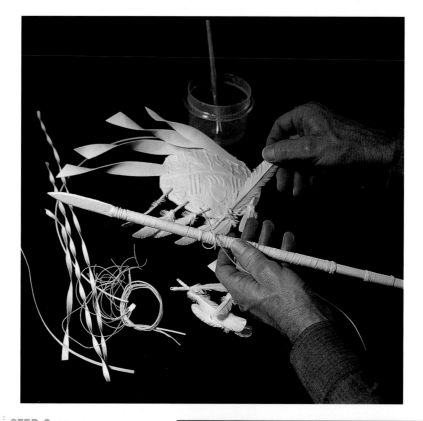

STEP 8 The bust is chased smooth and the face completed. Allen uses an exclusive process on his paper to make it look like leather. The figure here is being draped with this special leathery paper.

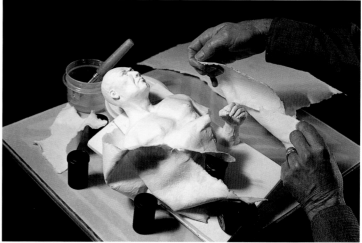

STEP 9 Another Eckman process creates the hair for his Wind Warrior. Here he is layering the hair into position. The bust has been remounted on the sculpture stand to add this detail.

STEP 10 Once the figure has dried, the lance and shield are added. The lance has been cut in half and slipped into the grasping hand. A paper dowel is used to reconnect the two pieces. Finally, feathers adorn the head. The finished work will be framed in a Plexiglas box. By using the Eckman method of reusable molds and altered casts, each piece in the Wind Warriors series becomes a one-of-a-kind original.

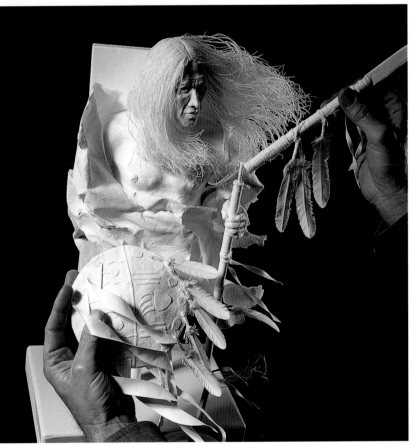

Four Claws in the Wind
Allen Eckman
20" x 16" x 5" (51 cm x 41 cm x 13 cm)

Sitting Bull's Vision

9' x 6'6" x 18" (2.7 m x 2 m x 46 cm)

Cast-paper sculpture.

The unfettered look of the eagle belies the careful work that goes into detailing the feathers. Eckman makes a sheet mold for casting the paper feathers, each of which is cut out, shaped, and hand-detailed before it is applied. More than 3,000 individually cast and applied paper feathers were used to finish the eagle.

Desperate Determination

36" x 60" x 12" (91 cm x 152 cm x 30 cm)

The mane of the buffalo was created by scraping a razor blade against the surface of a sheet of Eckman's handmade paper, producing a woolly mass that was then applied to the sculpture. Not all handmade papers produce this effect; you will need to experiment with different papers.

Wolf Spirit Vision Shield
40" x 28" x 7" (102 cm x 71 cm x 18 cm)
Cast-paper sculpture.

Confederate Cavalry Colonel
19" x 5" x 4" (48 cm x 13 cm x 10 cm)
Cast-paper sculpture.

Prairie Edge: The Chief and His Clan
60" x 84" (152 cm x 213 cm)
Dedicated to daughter, Michelle Eckman, who passed away on
April 30, 1994.
Cast-paper sculpture.

Pow Wow Practice (Mother and Daughter)
Approximately 17" x 20" x 11" (43 cm x 51 cm x 28 cm)
Cast-paper sculpture.

All art this and facing page: Allen Eckman

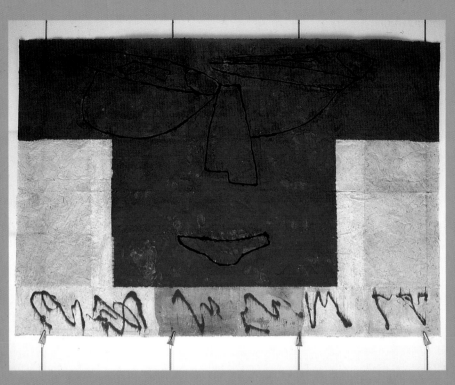

Anne Vilsbøll
Denmark
The Lioness
6 ½' x 10' (2 m x 3 m)
Handmade paper.

PULP PAPER

Gallery

Anne Vilsbøll
Denmark
Lion d'Or
6 ½' x 10' (2 m x 3 m)
Handmade paper.

Michael G. LaFosse
United States
Strombus Gallus III
30" (76 cm)
A lay-up of handmade Abaca paper,
calcium carbonate, and acrylic medium.

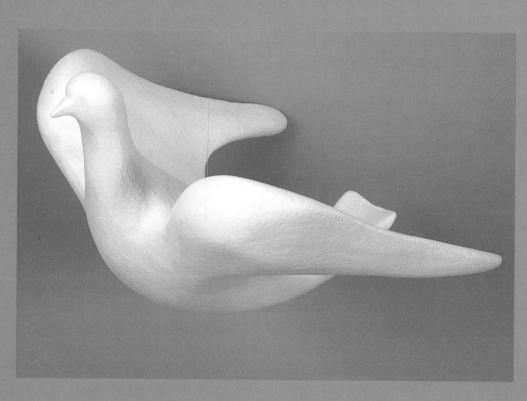

Richard L. Alexander
United States
Of Peace
12" x 16" (30 cm x 41 cm)
Over-beaten, high-shrinkage Abaca
pulp over sculpted polystyrene foam.

Resources

EDUCATIONAL PROGRAMS

Carriage House Paper/Massachusetts
8 Evans Road
Brookline, MA 02146
Phone: (617) 232-1636
Fax: (617) 277-7719
E-mail: paperroad@aol.com

Carriage House Paper/New York
79 Guernsey Street
Brooklyn, NY 11222
Phone/Fax: (718) 599-7857

Columbia College Chicago Center for Book & Paper Arts
218 South Wabash Avenue, 7th Floor
Chicago, IL 60604-2316
Phone: (312) 431-8612
Fax: (312) 986-8237

Dieu Donné Papermill, Inc.
433 Broome Street
New York, NY 10013
Phone: (212) 226-0573
Fax: (212) 226-6088
E-mail: ddpaper@cybernex.net

Eckman Fine Art
222 Timberline Court
Rapid City, SD 57702
Phone: (605) 343-4252

Origamido Studio
63 Wingate Street
Haverhill, MA 01832
Phone: (508) 372-1215
E-mail: michael@origamido.com

Twinrocker
P.O. Box 413
Brookston, IN 47923
Phone: (800) 757-8946

ORGANIZATIONS

IAPMA (International Association of Hand Papermakers and Paper Artists)
Anne Vilsbøll, President
Fredensgade 4
Strynø, Rudkøbing
DK-5900 Denmark

International Origami Society
P.O. Box 3
Ogikubo, Tokyo
167 Japan

Origami USA
15 West 77th Street
New York, NY 10024-5192
Phone: (212) 769-5635
Fax: (212) 769-5668

British Origami Society

c/o Penny Groo

2A The Chestnuts

Countesthorpe, Leicester

LE8 5TL England

Korea Jongi Jupgi Association

Institute of Paper Culture

5F Sukama Building 189

Dongsoong-Dong, Jongno-ku

Seoul, Korea

SUPPLIES

Carriage House Paper/New York

79 Guernsey Street

Brooklyn, NY 11222

Phone/Fax: (718) 599-7857

Dieu Donné Papermill, Inc.

433 Broome Street

New York, NY 10013

Phone: (212) 226-0573

Fax: (212) 226-6088

E-mail: ddpaper@cybernex.net

Fascinating Folds

Phone: (800) 968-2418

E-mail: sales@fascinating-folds.com

Gold's Artworks Inc.

2100 North Pine Street

Lumberton, NC 28358

Phone: (919) 739-9605

Lee Scott McDonald, Inc.

P.O. Box 264

Charlestown, MA 02129

Phone: (617) 242-2505

Fax: (617) 242-8825

Magnolia

2527 Magnolia Street

Oakland, CA 94607

Phone: (510) 839-5268

Fax: (510) 893-8334

Origami Source

c/o Phyliss Meth

40-05 166th Street

Flushing, NY 11358

Fax: (718) 762-2177

Paper Connection International

Lauren Pearlman

208 Pawtuxet Avenue

Cranston, RI 02905

Phone/Fax: (401) 461-2135

Rugg Road Paper Company

105 Charles Street

Boston, MA 02114

Phone: (617) 742-0002

Fax: (617) 742-0008

Twinrocker

P.O. Box 413

Brookston, IN 47923

Phone: (800) 757-8946

WEBSITES

The World Wide Web is a great resource for finding fellow artists, supply sources, and information. Using a web browser to enter key words such as "paper," "sculpture," "art," and "origami," you can call upon thousands of interesting websites. Below are some of our website preferences, each of which has links to other related sites. It is best to visit your favorite sites regularly to keep up to date—the address and content of many websites often change.

The Collector's Guide: Handmade Paper
A look at the handmade paper process and how four artists uniquely use paper as a medium.
http://www.collectorsguide.com/fa/fa022.html

Eckman Fine Art
http://www.eckmanfineart.com

Fascinating Folds
An extensive website featuring supplies and reference materials for paper art and crafts.
http://www.fascinating-folds.com

Handmade Paper
Information on all aspects of handmade paper and paper sculpture, with many links to related sites.
http://members.aol.com/handpaper/index.html

Handmade Paper Sculptures by Kara Young
http://www.world-web.com/crafts/mixed/karay01.htm

Handmade paper fish and other sea creatures by Duane and Sharon Rucker-Wurst
http://www.netstreetfair.com/010.html

Hummingbird Paper & Art
The home of creations made by handmade paper artist Heather R. Hiner.
http://members.aol.com/~paperart/index.html

Joseph Wu's Origami Page
The mother of all origami web page— includes many links.
http://www.origami.net/homes/jwu/
http://www.datt.co.jp/origami

Mary Kay Colling Gallery
Printmaker/Papermaker Village
Cast paper relief, paper sculpture, and graphics for home and office walls.
http://mkcolling.com/

Origamido
Michael G. LaFosse and Alexander, Blace and Company's origami videotape productions.
http://www.origamido.com

Origami Network
Provides links to other origami websites.
http://www.origami.net

Origami USA Home Page

A volunteer-based, nonprofit, cultural, and educational arts organization of origami enthusiasts from around the world.

http://www.origami-usa.org/

Paper Art

Paper art made by indigenous and creative people of the world.

http://www.folkart.com/~latitude/home/paper.htm

Patti's Sculptures and Other Art!

http://www.nmia.com/~dsully/patti/index.html

Paws & Reflect

Handmade paper creations from the studio of Cris Zack and Andrea Hedrick.

http://kcd.com/ravenswindow/paws.htm

Pondside Pulp and Paper

A source for handmade paper, handmade paper products, and workshops on making paper and artist's books.

http://members.aol.com/tylerpaper/pondside.html

The Progressive Art Center & Gallery Classroom

Offers a wide variety of classes to students of all ages.

http://www.internet-95.com/company/pacg/class.htm

Starcatcher Paper Sculpture

Cast paper vessels and handmade paper-covered basketry by Pat Baldwin.

http://membrane.com/~catcher/

Tosa Washi *Japanese Paper Museum*

http://202.32.254.20/~stranger/yosakoi/washi.htm

Twinrocker Handmade Paper On-Line

http://dcwi.com/~twinrock/Welcome.html

ZinaPapers

Handmade papers and art. Visit the paper studio to see floral, decorative, and garden papers.

http://www1.shore.net/~zina/

Directory of Artists

Richard L. Alexander
170 Margin Street
Haverhill, MA 01832-5109
Phone: (508) 373-5645
Fax: (508) 373-5503
E-mail: Richard@origamido.com

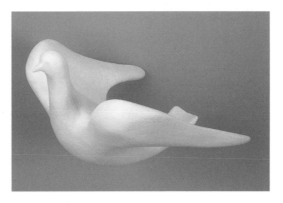

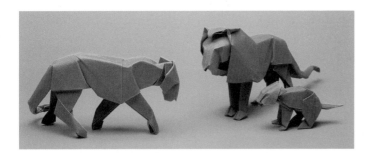

David Brill
3 Worth Hall
Middlewood Road
Poynton, Stockport
Cheshire
SK12 1TS England

Sara Peoria Burr
21 Bothwell Road
Brighton, MA 02135

Allen Eckman
222 Timberline Court
Rapid City, SD 57702
Phone: (605) 343-4252
E-mail: allen@eckmanfineart.com

Patty Tenneboe-Eckman
222 Timberline Court
Rapid City, SD 57702
Phone: (605) 343-4252
E-mail: patty@eckmanfineart.com

Dan Fletcher
4761 Broadway, #2E
New York, NY 10034
Phone: (212) 304-4602
E-mail: DPFB@aol.com

Tomoko Fuse
Yasakamura
Kitaazumi-gun
Nagano-ken
399-73 Japan

Helen Hiebert
493 3rd Street
Brooklyn, NY 11215

Lisa Houck
535 Albany Street
Unit 3, 4th Floor
Boston, MA 02118
Phone: (617) 338-4748

Paul Jackson
21 Hardwicke Road
London
N13 4SL England

Eric Joisel
22 Rue Louis Delamarre
Enghien-les-Bains
95880 France

Donna Koretsky
79 Guernsey Street
Brooklyn, NY 11222
Phone/Fax: (718) 599-7857

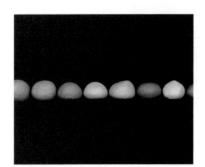

Michael G. LaFosse

170 Margin Street
Haverhill, MA 01832-5109
Phone: (508) 373-5645
Fax: (508) 373-5503
E-mail: michael@origamido.com

Robert J. Lang

7580 Olive Drive
Plesanton, CA 94588
E-mail: rjlang@aol.com

Kyoko Nakanishi

3-12-21 Midoricho
Tokorozawa, Saitama
359, Japan

Catherine Nash

1102 West Huron Street
Tucson, AZ 85745
Phone: (520) 740-1673

Directory of Artists

Calvin Nicholls
48 Bond Street
Lindsay, Ontario
K9V 3R2 Canada

Chris K. Palmer
6980 Woodchuck Hill Road
Fayatteville, NY 13066
Phone: (315) 445-1589

Naomiki Sato
21, Rue de Meaux
Paris
75019 France

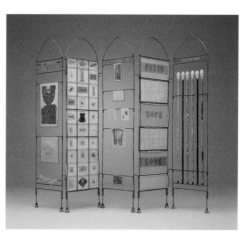

Joan M. Soppe
Nom de Plume Studio
716 Oakland Road Northeast
Cedar Rapids, IA 52402

Anne Vilsbøll
Fredensgade 4
Strynø, Rudkøbing
DK-5900 Denmark

Hermann van Goubergen
Hof Van Tichelen 38
2020
Antwerp
Belgium

Akira Yoshizawa
P.O. Box 3
Ogikubo, Tokyo
167 Japan

Joe Zina
One Fitchburg Street B154
Somerville, MA 02143
Phone: (617) 625-7007
Fax: (617) 776-3067
E-mail: Jzina@aol.com

Acknowledgments

It has been a wonderful experience to get to know the many fine artists represented in this collection. I am indebted to them for their generosity in sharing their creations and methods, and I thank them for their kind attention to my many requests for text and materials. I am grateful to Shawna Mullen and Rockport Publishers for this assignment, which has made it all possible.

I also wish to thank the following people for lending their talent and courteous help in the production of this book: Martha Wetherill, for working closely with me and for patiently reviewing, editing, and refining the manuscript; Richard Alexander, for jumping in at the keyboard from time to time and for all of his timely advice about this project; Michael Lafferty, for his fine work on the bulk of the studio and gallery photography, and for his patience and good humor on the set; and Lynne Havighurst, Sandee Havunen, and Heather Yale, for their artistic talent, art direction, and enthusiasm, which brought out the best the team had to give.

I am deeply indebted to my friend Mrs. Emiko Kruckner, who has been my liaison to origami master Akira Yoshizawa, making it possible for my mentor to be included in this book.

The help of these and many other talented people has made the creation of this beautiful and worthwhile book both an honor and a pleasure.

Photography by Michael Lafferty as follows: Materials, project, and gallery photos for Michael G. LaFosse and Chris K. Palmer; materials and project photos for Akira Yoshizawa and Sara Burr; gallery photos for Richard L. Alexander, Eric Joisel, Robert J. Lang, and Naomiki Sato.

Additional photography credited as follows: Materials and project photos for Lisa Houck by Kevin Thomas, gallery photos by Clements Howcroft Photography; photos of Catherine Nash's "Homage to Magnani" by Robert Renfrow; materials and project photos for Joe Zina and photo of Joe Zina's "Man's Thoughts" by Kevin Thomas: gallery photos for David Brill by Neil Mcallister; gallery photos for Joan M. Soppe by Mike Schlotter. All other photographs were taken by the artist, or the photographer's name was not available at press time.

The procedures and images shown in the sections on Patty Eckman and Allen Eckman are protected by copyright law.

Credits

About the Author

Michael G. LaFosse, most widely known for his original work in origami, the art of paper folding, is regarded as an American master of the art. His creative work in paper sculpture and papermaking began when he was sixteen. Japanese origami master Akira Yoshizawa can be credited for stirring Michael's passion for designing folded works that capture the character of nature's creatures. Michael also develops geometric and modular origami, and gets regular exercise while perfecting any of the hundreds of original paper airplanes he has designed.

With many exhibits and collaborations to his credit, Michael enjoys the works of others as much as creating his own. He travels widely, studying nature and teaching groups of students in schools, universities, community libraries, museums, and conventions.

Michael G. LaFosse's Origamido Studio, just north of Boston, is a teaching and exhibit space for origami art, as well as a papermaking and working studio for creating designs in handmade paper. Michael's folding designs are available through the productions of Alexander, Blace & Company.